COCKTAILS

COCKTAILS

shaken & stirred

MARK HARRISON

NEW HOLLAND

contents

METHODS OF MIXING COCKTAILS

The methods below are the most common processes of mixing cocktails:-

SHAKE AND STRAIN

To 'shake' means to mix a cocktail by shaking it in a cocktail shaker by hand. Shakers make it easy and practical to mix ingredients that do not combine easily with spirits, such as juices, egg whites, cream and sugar syrups.

Most shakers have two or three parts. First, fill the main part of the shaker three-quarters full with ice, then pour the ingredients on top of the ice. Less expensive ingredients should be poured before deluxe ingredients. Replace the lid or cap and shake vigorously for 10–15 seconds. Remove the cap or top part of the shaker and, using a Hawthorn strainer – the shaker's own built-in strainer – or a knife, strain the contents into the cocktail glass. This technique prevents the ice from decanting into the glass, protecting the cocktail and ensuring the melted ice doesn't dilute the flavour and mixture.

If you misplace the shaker cap, a coaster or the inside palm of your hand is quite effective. To sample the cocktail before serving to the customer, pour a small amount into the shaker cap and use a straw to check the taste.

SHAKE AND POUR

After shaking the cocktail, pour the contents straight into the glass, without straining out the ice. This technique is used when pouring into hi-ball glasses and sometimes old-fashioned spirit glasses.

STIR AND STRAIN

To 'stir' a cocktail means to mix the ingredients by stirring them with ice in a mixing glass and then straining them into a chilled cocktail glass. The stirring motion requires short, circular twirls. Spirits, liqueurs and vermouths that blend easily together are mixed by this method.

BUILD

To 'build' a cocktail means to mix the ingredients in the glass in which the cocktail is to be served, pouring one on top of the other. Hi-ball, long fruit juice and carbonated mixed cocktails are typically built using this technique. The drink should be served with a swizzle stick so that the customer can stir the ingredients. Long straws are excellent substitutes when swizzle sticks are unavailable.

BLEND AND POUR

To 'blend' a cocktail means to mix the ingredients using an electric blender or mixer. Any fruit (fresh or canned) should be added first. Adding the fruit in small pieces gives a smoother texture than if you add the fruit whole. Next add the alcohol. Add the ice last. Working in this order ensures that the fruit is blended

Cocktails – fun and flamboyant drinks, served in fancy glasses and dressed to impress; drinks of unmistakable drama in which decadence and elegance combine.

thoroughly with the alcoholic ingredients before the ice chills the beverage.

Ideally, the ingredients should be blended for at least 20 seconds, in order to prevent ice and fruit lumps forming that will need to be strained out. If the blender starts to rattle or hum, ice may be obstructing the blades.

Always check that the blender is clean before you start. Angostura bitters is suitable as a cleaning agent. Add four to five shakes of Angostura to the blender, fill with hot water, rinse and then wipe clean.

LAYER OR FLOAT

Some ingredients are 'layered' or 'floated' on the surface of the cocktail. Usually these are ingredients that you do not wish to blend with other ingredients. To layer or float an ingredient, hold a bar spoon or dessert spoon the right way up and rest it with the lip slightly above the level of the last addition. Fill the spoon gently and the contents will flow smoothly from all around the rim on to the surface. Experienced bartenders use the back of the spoon.

MUDDLE

'Muddling' is the process of crushing or bruising fruit or mint garnishes in a glass with the muddler end of the bar spoon or with a pestle, often with some sugar and a small amount of liqueur. Other ingredients of the cocktail are added after muddling is complete. The muddling process extracts the maximum flavour from the fruit or mint. The drink can be strained after muddling, if desired.

COCKTAIL KNOW-HOW

GARNISHING

Cocktail mixing is an art, which is expressed in the preparation and presentation of the cocktail.

Simplicity is the most important notion to keep in mind when garnishing cocktails. Don't overdo the garnish: make it striking, but if you can't get near the cocktail to drink it, then you have failed. Many world-class cocktails are served simply with a slice of lemon, a twist of orange rind, or a single red cherry. Tall refreshing hi-balls may have more garnish as the glass is larger. Plastic animals, umbrellas, fans and a whole variety of novelty goods are now available to use as a garnish and add a lot of fun to the drink.

Long cocktails are usually served with a swizzle stick for additional mixing. It's customary to serve straws with highly garnished cocktails as well as with cocktails made for women in order to avoid lipstick rubbing off on the glass.

SUITABLE ADDITIONS

Almonds, slivered	Fruit, canned	Rockmelon
Apple juice	Jelly babies	Salt
Apricot conserve	Lemon juice	Strawberries
Banana	Lemons	Sugar
Blueberries	Lime juice	Sugar cubes
Carbonated water	Limes	Sugar syrup
Celery	Maraschino cherries	Tabasco sauce
Celery salt	Milk	Tomato
Chocolate flakes	Mint leaves	Vanilla ice cream
Cinnamon	Nutmeg	Worcestershire sauce
Coconut cream	Olives	
Cream	Orange and mango juice	
Crushed pineapple	Orange juice	
Cucumber	Orange segments	
Eggs, fresh	Pepper	
Flowers (assorted)	Pineapple, fresh	
Fruit nectar, canned	Pineapple juice	
Fruit pulps, canned	Red cocktail onions	

FROSTING

A glass rim can be frosted with salt or sugar to provide a decorative look and to enhance the drink experience. Mint leaves can also be frosted for garnishing. To frost a glass rim, first rub a lemon or orange slice around it until it is coated with juice. Use lemon if you want to frost the rim with salt and orange if you want to frost the rim with sugar. Next, holding the glass by the stem, place the rim on a plate containing salt or sugar and turn slightly so that the crystals adhere to the glass. Pressing the glass too deeply into the salt or sugar will result in chunks sticking to the glass.

To make a sugar frosting turn pink, coat the rim of the glass with a small amount of grenadine and then gently rub it in the sugar. The grenadine will absorb the sugar and turn it pink.

To frost mint leaves for garnishes, dip them in egg white and while wet gently push each side into a saucer containing caster (superfine) sugar.

HOW TO MAKE A DECORATIVE CROSS

Using a sharp knife, find the centre point of a short straw and slice through it. Push another short straw through the slit and position to create a cross. Arrange the cross over the cocktail surface but so it's not touching the liquid. Dusting over the surface with ground (powdered) nutmeg or other sprinkles. Remove the straw cross to reveal a cross pattern on the drink's surface. Use this technique to create a decorative pattern on the surface of creamy cocktails such as Brandy Alexanders.

SUGAR SYRUP

Sugar syrup is needed in a good cocktail bar as sugar will not dissolve easily in cold cocktails. To make sugar syrup, fill a cup or bowl (depending on how much you need) with granulated (white) sugar. Fill with boiling water and stir continuously until the sugar is fully dissolved. Refrigerate when cold. Keeps indefinitely, but cover to keep airtight.

SOUR MIX

Sour mix, is also known as bar mix, and is an important addition to many cocktails. To make sour mix, whisk one egg white until frothy in a grease-free medium-sized bowl. Mix in 7 oz (200 g) of sugar, followed by 8 fl oz (250 ml) water and 16 fl oz (475 ml) of lemon juice. Beat until the sugar is dissolved. The egg whites are optional, but will make the drinks slightly foamy. Will keep in a refrigerator for about a week.

Note: Cocktails, drinks and garnishes containing raw egg are unsuitable for elderly, pregnant women or those who are in ill health.

HANDLING FRUIT JUICES

Never leave juices, coconut cream or other ingredients in cans once open. Pour them into clean bottles, cap them and refrigerate them.

Empty 1¼ pint (750 ml) glass spirit bottles make great storage for fruit juices as you can attach a nip or free pourer to make it easier to pour the correct measurements. Before using the bottle, soak it in hot water to remove both the label and the flavour of the alcohol.

HANDLING ICE

Ice is a vital ingredient of most cocktails and must be clean and fresh at all times. Small cubes and flat chips of ice are perfect for chilling and mixing cocktails. Ice cubes with holes are inefficient. Wet ice, ice scraps and broken ice should only be used in blenders.

To crush ice, fold the required amount of ice into a clean linen cloth and smash it against a solid surface. Although slightly uncivilised, this is an effective method. Don't use a bottle to hit the ice as the process may shatter the bottle.

Alternatively, a blender may be used to crush ice. Half fill the blender with ice and then pour in cold water until it reaches the level of the ice. Blend for about 30 seconds, strain out the water and you will have perfectly crushed ice. Portable ice crushers can also be used.

Always use a scoop to collect the ice from an ice tray or bucket. Never pick up ice with your hands, as this is unhygienic. Shovelling a glass into an ice tray to gather ice can cause the glass to shatter and should be avoided.

It is important that the ice tray or bucket is clean before you put any ice into it, to ensure that the ice is kept clean.

STOCKING YOUR COCKTAIL BAR

ESSENTIAL EQUIPMENT

Bottle openers

Can-opener

Coasters and serviettes

Cocktail shaker

Free pourers

Hand cloths for cleaning
glasses

Hawthorn strainer

Ice bucket

Ice scoop

Knife, cutting board

Measures (jiggers)

Mixing glass

Moulinex electric blender

Scooper spoon (long
teaspoon)

Spoon with muddler

Swizzle sticks, straws

Waiter's friend corkscrew

GLASSES – HELPFUL HINTS

You can serve cocktails in any type of glass, but the better the quality, the cleaner, and more sparkling the glass, the better the appearance of the cocktail. Don't use scratched, marked or coloured glasses as they will deter from the appearance of the cocktail.

To polish clean glasses, hold each individually over a container of boiling water until the glass becomes steamy. Rub the glass in a circular motion with a clean linen cloth until it is polished and gleaming. If the glass has a stem, hold it there while polishing to avoid marking the bowl of the glass.

All cocktail glasses should be kept chilled in a refrigerator or filled with ice while you are preparing the cocktails. An appealing effect on a glass can be achieved by running the polished glass under cold water and then placing it in the freezer.

All types of glasses have been designed for a specific type of drink:
- Hi-ball glasses for long, cool, refreshing drinks.
- Cocktail glasses for novelty drinks.
- Champagne saucers for creamy after-dinner-style drinks.
- Spirit glasses and tumblers for classic mixed drinks.
- Shot glasses for short strong drinks that are drunk in one hit (shooting).

TYPES OF GLASSES

Beer mug	12 fl oz (340 ml)
Brandy balloon	23 fl oz (650 ml)
Champagne flute	5 fl oz (145 ml), 7 fl oz (200 ml)
Champagne saucer	5 fl oz (145 ml)
Cocktail glass	90 ml (3 fl oz), 5 fl oz (145 ml), 230 ml (8 fl oz)
Cordial glass (embassy)	1 fl oz (30 ml)
Cordial glass (Lexington)	generous 1 fl oz (30 ml)
Cordial glass (tall Dutch)	1½ fl oz (45 ml)
Fancy cocktail glass	7 fl oz (200 ml), 10 fl oz (285 ml)
Fancy highball glass	8 fl oz (230 ml), 12 fl oz (340 ml), 16 fl oz (460 ml)
Footed highball glass	10 fl oz (285 ml), 12 fl oz (340 ml)
Footed pilsener plass	10 fl oz (285 ml)
Hi-ball glass	8 fl oz (230 ml), 10 fl oz (285 ml), 12 fl oz (340 ml)
Hurricane glass	8 fl oz (230 ml), 16 fl oz (460 ml), 23 fl oz (650 ml)
Irish coffee glass	8 fl oz (230 ml)
Margarita glass	5 fl oz (145 ml), 12 fl oz (340 ml)
Martini glass	3 fl oz (90 ml), 4 fl oz (115 ml), 1½ fl oz (45 ml), 8 fl oz (230 ml)
Old-fashioned spirit glass	6 fl oz (170 ml), 7 fl oz (200 ml), 10 fl oz (285 ml)
Poco grande glass	14 fl oz (400 ml)
Prism rocks glass	10 fl oz (285 ml)
Salud grande glass	10 fl oz (285 ml)
Shot glass	1½ fl oz (45 ml)
Wine glass	1½ fl oz (45 ml), 7 fl oz (200 ml)

GLOSSARY OF LIQUEURS AND SPIRITS

ABSOLUT CITRON: A lemon-flavoured vodka.

ABSOLUT KURANT: A blackcurrant-flavoured vodka.

ADVOCAAT: A combination of fresh egg yolks, sugar, brandy, vanilla and spirit. The recommended shelf life is 12–15 months from manufacture.

AMARETTO: A subtle liqueur with a distinct almond flavour. Amaretto (di Galliano) is a well-known brand.

AMER PICON: A bitter liqueur made with orange peel, quinine, spices and herbs. It is often used as a digestif.

AMONTILLADO SHERRY: A smooth-bodied sherry, golden-brown in colour, and aged in oak casks to give it a mellow, nutty flavour.

ANGOSTURA BITTERS: An essential part of any bar. A unique flavouring with origins that date back to 1824. It contains a 'secret' blend of natural herbs and spices and is used as a flavouring agent in sweet and savoury dishes and drinks. It is low in sodium and calories.

ANISETTE LIQUEUR: A liqueur flavoured with anise oil.

APRICOT BRANDY: An apricot-flavoured liqueur.

AQUAVIT: A Scandinavian liquor with the flavour of caraway seeds.

ARMAGNAC: A brandy made in the demarcated region of Armagnac, France.

ARRACK: A spirit distilled from the fermented sap of toddy palms or from fermented molasses.

BACARDI: A light-bodied rum. See Rum.

BAILEYS IRISH CREAM: The largest selling liqueur in the world. It is a blend of Irish whiskey, dairy cream and other flavourings. It is a natural product.

BANANA LIQUEUR (LENA): A banana-flavoured liqueur.

BENEDICTINE: A brandy-based liqueur. The perfect end to a perfect meal. Serve straight, with ice, soda, or as part of a favourite cocktail.

BOURBON (WHISKEY): A type of whiskey from the USA with a smooth, easy flavour.

BRANDY: A smooth and mild spirit, mainly produced from the juice of grapes, which is considered a very smooth and palatable drink and ideal for mixing.

BUTTERSCOTCH SCHNAPPS: A butterscotch-flavoured liqueur.

CALVADOS: Fine apple brandy made in Normandy.

CAMPARI: A bitter Italian aperitif. Suitable both as a long or short drink, or as a key ingredient in many fashionable cocktails.

CASSIS: A rich purple liqueur that delivers the robust flavour and aroma of blackberries. Cassis lends itself to neat drinking or an endless array of delicious sauces and desserts.

CHAMBORD: A raspberry liqueur.

CHARTREUSE: A liqueur available in yellow or green. It is made by monks of the Carthusian order.

CHERI-SUISSE: A chocolate- and cherry-flavoured liqueur from Switzerland.

CHERRY ADVOCAAT: A morello cherry-flavoured, advocaat-based liqueur.

CHERRY BRANDY: Made from concentrated morello cherry juice with a small quantity of bitter almonds and vanilla added. Enjoyable as a neat drink before or after dinner. Excellent for mixers and topping for ice cream.

CHERRY HEERING: A popular dark-red cherry-flavoured liqueur made in Denmark. Known also as Peter Heering.

COCONUT LIQUEUR: A smooth liqueur with the exotic flavour of coconut and heightened with light-bodied white rum.

COINTREAU: A liqueur with the aromatic orange flavour of natural citrus fruits. A great mixer and delightful over ice.

CRÈME DE BANANA: Creamy yellow liqueur very similar to banana liqueur.

CRÈME DE CACAO DARK: A rich chocolate liqueur. Smooth and classy. Serve on its own, or mix for all kinds of delectable treats.

CRÈME DE CACAO WHITE: This liqueur delivers a powerful and full-bodied chocolate flavour. An excellent mixer when a chocolate flavour without colour is desired.

CRÈME DE CAFÉ: A sweet brown liqueur made from extracts of coffee.

CRÈME DE CASSIS: A blood-red, sweet, blackcurrant-flavoured liqueur.

CRÈME DE GRAND MARNIER: A very smooth-tasting premium blend of Grand Marnier and French cream. The orange/Cognac flavour blends beautifully with the cream.

CRÈME DE MENTHE GREEN: A liqueur with a clear peppermint flavour, reminiscent of a fresh and crisp winter's day in the mountains. An excellent mixer.

CRÈME DE MENTHE WHITE: As for Crème de Menthe Green, when colour is not required.

CURAÇAO BLUE: Slightly bitter liqueur based on natural citrus fruits. Same as Triple Sec but brilliant blue colour is added to make cocktails visually more exciting.

CURAÇAO ORANGE: Same as Curaçao Blue, but has a strong orange colour and flavour.

CURAÇAO RED: Same as Curaçao Blue, but has a strong red colour.

CURAÇAO TRIPLE SEC: Also known as White Curaçao. As for Blue Curaçao, but without colour. One of the most versatile liqueurs. It can be enjoyed with or without ice as a neat drink, and is used in more mixed cocktails than any other liqueur.

DRAMBUIE: A Scotch whisky liqueur. Made from a 'secret' recipe dating back to 1745. The names comes from *an dram buidheach* meaning 'the drink that satisfies'.

DUBONNET: A wine-based aperitif from France flavoured with spices and quinine.

FERNET BRANCA: A bitter, aromatic Italian spirit made from more than 40 herbs and spices, with a base of grape alcohol. Often served as a digestif.

FRANGELICO: A wild hazelnut liqueur from Italy. Contains infusions of berries and flowers to enrich the flavour.

GALLIANO (LIQUEUR): A classic golden liqueur that blends with a vast array of mixed drinks. Varieties include anise, licorice and vanilla.

GRAPPA: An Italian brandy made from distilling grape skins, known as a digestif.

GRENADINE CORDIAL: A grenadine-flavoured non-alcoholic syrup.

IRISH WHISKEY: The distinctive national whiskey of Ireland. Irish Whiskey is distilled three times, not twice. Made from malted barley, unmalted barley, and other grains such as rye and corn.

JÄGERMEISTER: This is a bitter German aperitif flavoured with a complex blend of 56 herbs, fruits and spices.

KAHLÚA: A smooth, dark Mexican liqueur made from real coffee and fine clear spirits.

GIN: A grain-based spirit with an aroma derived from juniper berries and other subtle herbs. The perfect mixer for short and long drinks.

GLAYVA: A whisky-based honey and herb-flavoured liqueur, similar to Drambuie.

GRAND MARNIER: An orange-flavour liqueur, an original blend of fine old Cognac and extract of oranges. The recipe is more than 150 years old.

KIRSCH: A fruit brandy distilled from morello cherries. Delicious drunk straight and excellent in a variety of food recipes.

MALIBU: A clear coconut liqueur based on white rum. Its distinctive taste blends naturally with virtually every mixer available.

MANDARIN NAPOLEON: A Belgian orange liqueur made from Cognac flavoured with oils from fresh Sicilian tangerines.

MANGO LIQUEUR (MOHALA): A mango-flavoured liqueur.

MELON LIQUEUR (MIDORI): A soft green liqueur that exudes a refreshing melon flavour. Smooth on the palate. Serve on the rocks, or use to create summertime cocktails.

MINT LIQUEUR: A term for any liqueur with mint flavouring, such as crème de menthe, peppermint schnapps, etc.

OPAL NERA: See Sambuca Black.

ORANGE BITTERS: Bitters made from unripe orange rinds infused in alcohol. See also Angostura Bitters.

ORANGE LIQUEUR: An orange-flavoured liqueur.

ORGEAT: A sweet almond-flavoured syrup made also with rose water and orange-flower water.

OUZO: The traditional aperitif of Greece. The distinctive flavour of this neutral grain spirit is derived mainly from the seed of the anise plant.

PARFAIT AMOUR: A light-bodied purple French liqueur made from lemons, oranges, brandy and herbs.

PASSIONFRUIT LIQUEUR (PASSOA): A passionfruit-flavoured liqueur.

PEACH LIQUEUR: The delicious flavour of fresh and dried peaches make this a cocktail lover's dream.

PEACHTREE SCHNAPPS: A crystal clear spirit, bursting with the taste of ripe peaches. Drink chilled, on the rocks or mix with any soft drink or juice.

PEAR BRANDY: A digestif made from pears, sometimes sold with a pear in the bottle.

PERNOD: A anise-flavoured French spirit, commonly drunk as an aperitif.

PIMM'S NO. 1 CUP: A gin-based liqueur, flavoured with a combination of herbs and spices.

PINEAPPLE LIQUEUR: A sun-filled delight. Delicious neat, a necessity for summer-time cocktails.

RUM: A spirit distilled from fermented sugar. Can be dark or light. A light-bodied rum is especially suited as a base for cocktails that require subtle aroma and delicate flavour.

RYE WHISKEY (CANADIAN CLUB): Distilled from rye, corn and malted barley. A light, mild and delicate whiskey, ideal for drinking straight or in mixed cocktails.

SABRA: An Israeli liqueur with a unique flavour derived from tangy Jaffa oranges, with a hint of chocolate.

SAMBUCA BLACK: As for clear Sambuca but flavoured with extracts of black elderberry. Opal Nera is a premium Sambuca. Also Galliano Sambuca Black.

SAMBUCA CLEAR: An Italian liqueur made from elderberries with a touch of anise. Also called Galliano Sambuca.

SCOTCH WHISKY (GRANT'S): The distinctive national spirit of Scotland. Made from malted barley and other grains.

SOUTHERN COMFORT: A sweet and full-bodied peach-flavoured liqueur based on Bourbon whiskey. Its recipe is a secret.

STRAWBERRY LIQUEUR (RUBIS): A fluorescent red liqueur with an unmistakable strawberry bouquet.

STREGA: From Italian origins, Strega is made from orange peel, spices and strong spirits. It is very sweet.

TENNESSEE WHISKEY (JACK DANIEL'S): A type of whiskey distinctive from Bourbon, made from the 'old sour mash' process. It is leached through hard maple charcoal, then aged in charred white oak barrels at a controlled temperature, in order to acquire its body, bouquet and colour, while remaining smooth.

TEQUILA: A spirit distilled from the sap of the agave or century plant. A perfect mixer or drink straight with salt and lemon.

TIA MARIA: A rum-based liqueur whose flavour derives from the finest Jamaican coffee. It is not too sweet with a subtle taste of coffee.

TRIPLE SEC: See Curaçao Triple Sec.

VANDERMINT: A rich chocolate liqueur with the added zest of mint.

VERMOUTH: Vermouth is a herbally-infused wine, made in France and Italy. Three styles are the most prevalent: Bianco, Rosso and Dry.

VERMOUTH BIANCO: A light, fruity and refreshing Vermouth. Mixes well with soda, lemonade and fruit juices.

VERMOUTH DRY: A crisp, light and dry Vermouth, used as a base for many cocktails.

VERMOUTH ROSSO: This Vermouth has a bittersweet herbal flavour, and is often drunk as an aperitif.

VODKA: The second best selling spirit in the world, generally made from grain or potatoes. Most vodkas are filtered through tanks containing charcoal to remove all odours and impurities. SKYY Vodka is a premium 40 per cent proof ABV vodka that is made from the finest American grain and 100 per cent filtered water. It is smooth-tasting and remarkably pure. Purity

was the objective of SKYY's creator, American entrepreneur Maurice Kanbar, who set out to remove all of the headache-causing impurities that form during the fermentation process and to remove the fusel oils so often found in vodka-type spirits.

WEST COAST COOLER: A white wine–based alcoholic drink with fruit flavours.

WHISKY, WHISKEY: See Bourbon whiskey, Irish whiskey, rye whiskey, Scotch whisky and Tennessee whiskey.

LAYERING OF DRINKS

Shooters (or pousse-cafés) are perhaps the most visually appealing drinks a barman can produce, especially when they are layered correctly. The secret is in the knowledge of the specific weight of the liqueur used. Lighter liqueurs rise to the top of the heavier ones. It therefore follows that the heaviest liqueurs are poured in the glass first and the lighter ones follow according to weight. The result is distinctive with each colorful liqueur appearing separate, one on top of the other. You will have to be very careful when pouring or layering as sometimes the weight of the liqueurs used is very similar and instead of a clear line you will get a very foggy mixture. To make the layering easier it is best to pour each liqueur over the rounded surface of a teaspoon, which has the effect of spreading the liqueur evenly over the one below without mixing them. When the glass used is too narrow to accommodate a spoon, insert a glass stirring rod into the glass and then slowly pour each liqueur in turn down the rod. This method, while slow, can be rewarding if similar weighted liqueurs are used. Always be very careful not to touch the inside of the glass while you pour.

As a general rule, the greater the alcohol content of the ingredient, the lighter the weight of the liquid. If you desire a large number of layers, start with dense alcohol-free syrups such as grenadine or coffee-flavouring, then finish with sweet cream.

It is important that you layer the drinks in this book exactly in the order given in the recipes.

Experiment and make your own beautiful cocktails by using the Liqueur Weight Guide below:

Crème de Cassis (50 proof)	1.18
Crème de Banana (50 proof)	1.18
Anisette Liqueur (red or white 50 proof)	1.17
Crème de Menthe White (60 proof)	1.16
Crème de Menthe Green (60 proof)	1.16
Crème de Cacao (brown or white 50 proof)	1.15
Gold Liqueur (50 proof)	1.15
Kahlúa	1.15
Coffee Liqueur (48 proof)	1.14
Maraschino Liqueur (50 proof)	1.14
Crème de Cacao White	1.14
Parfait Amour (50 proof)	1.13
Cherry Liqueur (48 proof)	1.12
Crème de Noyaux	1.12

Strawberry Liqueur	1.12
Blue Curaçao (60 proof)	1.11
Galliano	1.11
Amaretto	1.10
Blackberry Liqueur (50 proof)	1.10
Orange Curaçao	1.10
Apricot Liqueur (58 proof)	1.09
Cranberry Liqueur	1.09
Tia Maria	1.09
Green Chartreuse	1.09
Dry Orange Curaçao (60 proof)	1.09
Triple Sec (60 proof)	1.09
Drambuie	1.08
Frangelico	1.08
Sambuca (clear or black)	1.08
Coffee-flavoured Brandy (70 proof)	1.07
Liqueur Monastique (78 proof)	1.07
Peach-flavoured Brandy (70 proof)	1.07
Cherry-flavoured Brandy (70 proof)	1.07
Blackberry-flavoured Brandy (70 proof)	1.07
Apricot-flavoured Brandy (70 proof)	1.07
Campari	1.07
Midori Melon Liqueur	1.05
Rye Liqueur (60 proof)	1.05
Ginger-flavoured Brandy (70 proof)	1.05
Peppermint Schnappes (60 proof)	1.05
Kummel (78 proof)	1.05
Peach Liqueur (60 proof)	1.05
Sloe Gin (60 proof)	1.04
Benadictine	1.04
Grand Marnier	1.04
Brandy	1.04
Cointreau	1.04
Water	1.00
Tuaca	0.98
Southern Comfort	0.97
Kirsch	0.94

Aperitifs

By definition, an aperitif is an alcoholic drink taken as an appetizer before a meal. An aperitif is a fun and elegant drink that will help your guests to unwind and relax. An aperitif should tempt the palate and stimulate the tastebuds, whetting the appetite for the food and drink to follow. If you are having a cocktail party aperitifs can be wonderful conversation starters.

Allies Cocktail

INGREDIENTS
1 fl oz (30 ml) gin
1 fl oz (30 ml) dry vermouth
1 tsp (5 ml) lemon kümmel

GLASS
3 fl oz (90 ml) cocktail glass

Combine all the ingredients with ice in a mixing glass and stir well. Strain into the glass.

serves 1

Ante

INGREDIENTS
1 fl oz (30 ml) dubonnet rouge
1 fl oz (30 ml) Calvados
½ fl oz (15 ml) Cointreau

GLASS
3 fl oz (90 ml) cocktail glass

Combine all the ingredients with ice in a mixing glass and stir well. Strain into glass.

serves 1

Argincourt

INGREDIENTS
1 fl oz (30 ml) sweet vermouth
1 fl oz (30 ml) dry vermouth
½ fl oz (15 ml) amaretto
1 tsp (5 ml) lemon juice

GLASS
3 fl oz (90 ml) cocktail glass

Shake all the ingredients with ice and strain into a cocktail glass.

serves 1

Astoria

INGREDIENTS
1½ fl oz (45 ml) gin
1 fl oz (30 ml) dry vermouth
dash of orange bitters
1 olive, to garnish

GLASS
6 fl oz (170 ml) old-fashioned
    glass

Combine all the ingredients except for the olive in a mixing glass with ice and stir well. Strain into the serving glass, then drop the olive into the liquid.

serves 1

Bresnan

INGREDIENTS
1½ fl oz (45 ml) sweet
   vermouth
1 fl oz (30 ml) dry vermouth
½ fl oz (15 ml) lemon juice
1 tsp (5 ml) crème de cassis

GLASS
3 fl oz (90 ml) cocktail glass

Shake all the ingredients with ice and strain into the cocktail glass.

serves 1

Campari & Soda

INGREDIENTS
2 fl oz (60 ml) campari
2 fl oz (60 ml) soda water
1 slice of orange, to garnish

GLASS
6 fl oz (170 ml) old-fashioned
   glass

Build over ice and stir well. Garnish with the slice of orange.

serves 1

Cardicas

INGREDIENTS
1 fl oz (30 ml) light rum
½ fl oz (15 ml) Cointreau
½ fl oz (15 ml) port

GLASS
3 fl oz (90 ml) cocktail glass

Combine all the ingredients in a mixing glass with ice and stir well. Strain into the glass.

serves 1

Claridge's

INGREDIENTS
1 fl oz (30 ml) dry vermouth
1 fl oz (30 ml) gin
2 tsp (10 ml) apricot brandy
2 tsp (10 ml) Cointreau

GLASS
3 fl oz (90 ml) Champagne
saucer

Combine all the ingredients in a mixing glass with ice and stir well. Strain into the serving glass.

serves 1

Cynar Cocktail

INGREDIENTS
1 fl oz (30 ml) cynar
1 fl oz (30 ml) sweet vermouth
½ slice of orange, to garnish

GLASS
3 fl oz (90 ml) cocktail glass

Mix the liquid ingredients with 2–3 ice cubes in the glass.
Garnish with the orange slice on the side of the glass.

serves 1

Dry Negroni

INGREDIENTS
1 fl oz (30 ml) campari
1 fl oz (30 ml) gin
1 fl oz (30 ml) dry vermouth
lemon twist, to garnish

GLASS
6 fl oz (170 ml) old-fashioned
    spirit glass

Combine all the liquid ingredients in a glass almost filled with
ice and stir well. Garnish with the lemon twist dropped into
the glass.

serves 1

Dunlop

INGREDIENTS
1½ fl oz (45 ml) light rum
1 fl oz (30 ml) dry sherry
dash of Angostura bitters
1 piece lemon peel, to garnish

GLASS
3 fl oz (90 ml) cocktail glass

Combine all the liquid ingredients in a mixing glass with ice and stir well. Strain into the serving glass. Squeeze lemon peel over the drink then add the peel to the glass.

serves 1

Gilia

INGREDIENTS
1½ fl oz (45 ml) aperol
1 fl oz (30 ml) Scotch whisky

GLASS
3 fl oz (90 ml) cocktail glass

Combine all the ingredients in a mixing glass with ice and stir well. Strain into the glass and serve with a stirrer.

serves 1

Imperial

INGREDIENTS
1 fl oz (30 ml) gin
1 fl oz (30 ml) dry vermouth
dash of Angostura bitters
dash of maraschino liqueur
1 olive, to garnish

GLASS
3 fl oz (90 ml) cocktail glass

Shake all the liquid ingredients with ice and strain into the cocktail glass. Spear the olive with a cocktail stick and add to the glass.

serves 1

Little Princess

INGREDIENTS
1 fl oz (30 ml) light rum
1 fl oz (30 ml) sweet vermouth
3 maraschino cherries, to garnish

GLASS
generous 5 fl oz (150 ml) tumbler

Combine all the liquid ingredients in a mixing glass with ice and stir well. Strain into the glass. Spear 3 cherries with a cocktail stick and arrange across the glass.

serves 1

Parisian

INGREDIENTS
1 fl oz (30 ml) gin
1 fl oz (30 ml) dry vermouth
2 tsp (10 ml) crème de cassis
lemon twist, to garnish

GLASS
3 fl oz (90 ml) cocktail glass

Combine all liquid ingredients with cracked ice in a cocktail shaker and shake well. Strain into a chilled glass and garnish with the lemon twist.

serves 1

Red Gin

INGREDIENTS
1½ fl oz (45 ml) gin
2 tsp (10 ml) cherry brandy
1 slice of orange, to garnish

GLASS
3 fl oz (90 ml) cocktail glass

Shake all the liquid ingredients with ice and strain into the cocktail glass. Garnish with the slice of orange speared with a cocktail stick.

serves 1

Robson

INGREDIENTS
1 fl oz (30 ml) dark rum
½ fl oz (15 ml) grenadine
½ fl oz (15 ml) orange juice
2 tsp (10 ml) lemon juice

GLASS
3 fl oz (90 ml) cocktail glass

Shake all the ingredients with ice and strain into the cocktail glass.

serves 1

Shaft

INGREDIENTS
1 fl oz (30 ml) aperol
1 fl oz (30 ml) gin
dry sparkling wine for
    topping up
½ slice of orange, to garnish

GLASS
10 fl oz (285 ml) hi-ball glass

Mix the aperol and gin with ice cubes in a hi-ball glass. Top up with the sparkling wine. Garnish the rim of the glass with the orange slice and serve with a straw and stirrer.

serves 1

South Express

INGREDIENTS
1 fl oz (30 ml) kirsch
1 fl oz (30 ml) dry vermouth
1 fl oz (30 ml) sweet vermouth
lemon zest, to garnish

GLASS
5 fl oz (145 ml) cocktail glass

Combine all the liquid ingredients in a mixing glass with ice and stir well. Strain into the glass. Garnish with lemon zest.

serves 1

Velvet & Silk

INGREDIENTS
1 fl oz (30 ml) cynar
1 fl oz (30 ml) gin
slice of lemon, to garnish

GLASS
3 fl oz (90 ml) cocktail glass

Shake all the liquid ingredients with ice and strain into the cocktail glass. Drop the lemon slice into the glass to garnish.

serves 1

Classics

No cocktail book would be complete without these time-honoured elegant originals. The favourites of the early jet set and the rat pack alike, these are cocktails that you could imagine being served on the first trans-Atlantic passenger flights. These drinks were show-stopping spectacles in the bars of all of the major cities of the world – a celebration of New World sophistication, the traditional manufacture of exotic spirits and the inventiveness of blending flavours.

Bloody Mary

INGREDIENTS
1 fl oz (30 ml) vodka
4 fl oz (120 ml) tomato juice
dash of Worcestershire sauce
few drops of Tabasco
salt and black pepper

1 stalk celery, to garnish
1 stick cucumber, to garnish
slice of lemon, to garnish

GLASS
9 fl oz (285 ml) hi-ball glass

Shake the liquid ingredients and salt and pepper over ice and pour into the glass. Garnish with celery, cucumber and the slice of lemon.

serves 1

Brandy Alexander

INGREDIENTS
1 fl oz (30 ml) brandy
1 fl oz (30 ml) dark crème de
    cacoa
1 fl oz (30 ml) double (heavy)
    cream

ground (powdered) nutmeg
1 cherry, to garnish

GLASS
5 fl oz (145 ml) cocktail glass

Shake all the ingredients except the nutmeg and cherry with the ice and strain into the glass. Garnish with nutmeg. Slide the cherry onto the cocktail stick and add to the glass.

serves 1

Champagne Cocktail

INGREDIENTS
1 sugar cube
6 drops Angostura bitters
½ fl oz (15 ml) Cognac
4 fl oz (120 ml) Champagne

1 cherry, to garnish

GLASS
5 fl oz (145 ml) Champagne
flute

Soak the sugar cube in the Angostura bitters in the flute before adding the Cognac, then top with Champagne. Drop the cherry into the glass.

serves 1

Cosmopolitan

INGREDIENTS
1½ fl oz (45 ml) vodka
1 fl oz (30 ml) Cointreau
1 fl oz (30 ml) cranberry juice
½ fl oz (15 ml) freshly squeezed
    lime juice
wedge of lime, to garnish

GLASS
5 fl oz (145 ml) cocktail glass

Combine the liquid ingredients in a cocktail shaker with cracked ice and shake well. Pour into a chilled glass. Garnish with the lime wedge.

serves 1

Daiquiri

INGREDIENTS
1½ fl oz (45 ml) white rum
1 fl oz (30 ml) freshly squeezed
  lemon juice
½ fl oz (15 ml) sugar syrup (see
  introduction)
½ egg white (optional)
lemon twist, to garnish

GLASS
5 fl oz (145 ml) Champagne
  saucer

Shake all the ingredients except for the lemon spiral with
ice and strain into the Champagne saucer. Garnish with the
lemon twist.

serves 1

Death in the Afternoon

INGREDIENTS
½ fl oz (15 ml) Pernod
4 fl oz (120 ml) Champagne

GLASS
5 fl oz (145 ml) Champagne
  flute

Pour the Pernod into glass then fill with chilled Champagne.

serves 1

Fluffy Duck

INGREDIENTS
1 fl oz (30 ml) white rum
1 fl oz (30 ml) advocaat
lemonade
1¾ fl oz (40 ml) double (heavy)
    cream
slice of orange, to garnish
1 red cherry, to garnish

GLASS
9 fl oz (285 ml) fancy hi-ball
    glass

Build over ice and top up with lemonade to about a finger-width from the top of the glass, then float the cream on top. Garnish with the orange slice and red cherry.

serves 1

Gibson

INGREDIENTS
2¼ fl oz (60 ml) gin
½ fl oz (15 ml) dry vermouth
1 white cocktail onion, to garnish

GLASS
3 fl oz (90 ml) cocktail glass

Pour the gin and vermouth into glass over ice and stir. Pierce the onion with a cocktail stick and drop into the drink.

serves 1

Godfather

INGREDIENTS
1 fl oz (30 ml) Scotch whisky
1 fl oz (30 ml) amaretto

GLASS
7 fl oz (200 ml) old-fashioned
 glass

Pour the liquid into the glass over ice and stir.

serves 1

Harvey Wallbanger

INGREDIENTS
1 fl oz (30 ml) vodka
½ fl oz (15 ml) Galliano
4 fl oz (120 ml) orange juice
½ slice of orange, to garnish

1 red cherry, to garnish

GLASS
9 fl oz (285 ml) fancy hi-ball
 glass

Build over ice and top up with orange juice. Garnish with the orange slice and cherry.

serves 1

Long Island Iced Tea

INGREDIENTS

1 fl oz (30 ml) vodka
1 fl oz (30 ml) tequila
1 fl oz (30 ml) white rum
½ fl oz (15 ml) Cointreau
1 fl oz (30 ml) lemon juice
1 fl oz (30 ml) sugar syrup (see
   introduction)

dash of cola
lemon twist
mint leaves, to garnish

GLASS

9 fl oz (285 ml) fancy hi-ball
   glass

Build over ice and top up with cola. Garnish with the lemon
twist and mint leaves. Serve with a straw and stirrer.

serves 1

Manhattan

INGREDIENTS

1½ fl oz (45 ml) Bourbon
1 fl oz (30 ml) sweet vermouth
dash of Angostura bitters
1 red cherry, to garnish

GLASS

5 fl oz (145 ml) cocktail glass

Pour into glass over ice and stir, then strain into a clean glass.
Garnish with the cherry on a cocktail stick.

serves 1

Mint Julep

INGREDIENTS
1 tsp (5 ml) sugar
3 dashes of soda water
5 sprigs fresh mint
2 fl oz (60 ml) Bourbon

GLASS
9 fl oz (285 ml) fancy hi-ball
  glass

Muddle the sugar, soda water and 4 mint sprigs in a
glass. Pour into a chilled glass packed with ice. Add Bourbon
and mix with a chopping motion using a long-handled bar spoon.
Garnish with the remaining mint and serve with a straw.

serves 1

Old–Fashioned Scotch

INGREDIENTS
Angostura bitters
1 sugar cube
1 fl oz (30 ml) Scotch whisky
soda water
slice of lemon, to garnish
slice of orange, to garnish

GLASS
7 fl oz (200 ml) old-fashioned
  glass

Splash bitters evenly over sugar cube before adding ice and
Scotch. Top up with soda water. Garnish with the slice of
lemon and orange.

serves 1

Orgasm

INGREDIENTS
1 fl oz (30 ml) Baileys
1 fl oz (30 ml) Cointreau
1 strawberry, to garnish

GLASS
4 fl oz (145 ml) Champagne
flute

Pour the liquid ingredients into the glass over ice and stir.
Garnish with the strawberry on the side.

serves 1

Rusty Nail

INGREDIENTS
1 fl oz (30 ml) Scotch whisky
1 fl oz (30 ml) drambuie
lemon twist, to garnish

GLASS
7 fl oz (200 ml) old-fashioned
glass

Build over ice. Garnish with the lemon.

serves 1

Screwdriver

INGREDIENTS
1½ fl oz (45 ml) vodka
1½ fl oz (45 ml) orange juice
slice of orange, to garnish

GLASS
7 fl oz (200 ml) old-fashioned
   glass

Build over ice. Garnish with the orange.

serves 1

Whisky Sour

INGREDIENTS
1½ fl oz (45 ml) Scotch whisky
1 fl oz (30 ml) lemon juice
½ fl oz (15 ml) sugar syrup
   (see introduction)
½ egg white

slice of lemon, to garnish
1 red cherry, to garnish

GLASS
5 fl oz (145 ml) old-fashioned
   wine glass

Shake all the ingredients except for the lemon slice and
cherry over ice, then strain into the glass. Garnish with the
lemon and drop in the cherry.

serves 1

THE MARGARITA

The history of the Mexican margarita cocktail is highly romanticised and there are a number of theories that explain its origins. Several are rather convincing, including:
• It was created at the Caliente Race Track in Tijuana in the early 1930s.
• In 1936 Danny Negrete invented the drink for his girlfriend, Margarita, while he was working at the Hotel Garcia Crespo.
• In 1938, Carlos Herrera invented the drink for Marjorie King, who apparently couldn't drink anything except tequila.
• On 4 July 1942, a customer requested a Magnolia from barman Francisco Morales. However, he couldn't remember the recipe, so made up another drink and called it Daisy instead. (Daisy is Mexican for margarita.)
• In the 1940s, Enrique Bastante Gutierrez created the drink for Rita Hayworth, whose real name was Margarita Carmen Cansino.
• In 1948 Margaret Sames created the drink for a special party.
• In 1948 it was created in Galveston, Texas, by Santos Cruz, who mixed it for Peggy Lee.
• In the early 1950s it was created at the Tail o' the Cock restaurant in Los Angeles in order to find a way to introduce Jose Cuervo tequila into the market.

MIXING MARGARITAS

The golden rule when assembling this cocktail, is to use a proper ratio of the ingredients used, in order to present a balance of flavours. A perfect margarita is tart and not too sweet. It is served ice-cold in a salt-rimmed margarita glass. There are many serving variations including straight-up, on-the-rocks and frozen, all of them giving the recipient a wonderful taste sensation and each perfect to drink on a hot afternoon or evening. For best results use 3 parts tequila, 2 parts triple sec and 1 part freshly squeezed lime juice. Always make sure that you have clean ice cubes and plenty of them!

THE INGREDIENTS

For mixed cocktails you don't need to run to the expense of buying top quality brand spirits to get an acceptable result. I like to use Jose Cuervo blanco/silver tequila with Cointreau as the ideal triple sec, and I always choose fresh limes. You could use bottled juice but freshly squeezed fruit has a better taste. Look for limes that give a little when you squeeze them because they are juicer. Darker limes have a stronger flavour then the lighter ones. .

Traditional Margarita

INGREDIENTS
2 slices of lemon
salt
1 fl oz (30 ml) tequila
1 fl oz (30 ml) lemon juice
½ fl oz (15 ml) Cointreau

½ egg white (optional)

GLASS
5 fl oz (145 ml) margarita glass

Rub the rim of the glass with 1 slice of lemon and frost with salt. Shake all ingredients except lemon with ice and strain into glass. Garnish with remaining lemon slice on side of glass.

serves 1

Apple Margaritas

INGREDIENTS
lemon slice
1 fl oz (30 ml) lemon juice
salt
1 fl oz (30 ml) tequila
1 fl oz (30 ml) Calvados

1 fl oz (30 ml) Grand Marnier
   Rouge
1 fl oz (30 ml) grenadine
lemon slices, to garnish

GLASS
7 fl oz (200 ml) cocktail glass

Rub the margarita glass rims with the lemon slice and frost
with salt. Combine liquid ingredients with ice; shake well.
Strain into prepared glasses. Garnish each glass with a lemon
slice and serve.

serves 3

Banana Margarita

INGREDIENTS
lemon or lime slice
1 fl oz (30 ml) banana liqueur
salt
½ fl oz (15 ml) Cointreau
1½ fl oz (45 ml) tequila

1 fl oz (30 ml) lime or lemon
   juice
banana slice, to garnish

GLASS
5 fl oz (145 ml) margarita glass

Rub the margarita glass rim with lime or a lemon juice and
frost with salt. Combine the liquid ingredients with ice; shake
well. Strain the drink into the glass. Garnish with banana slice
and serve.

serves 1

Blackberry Margarita

INGREDIENTS
lemon or lime slice
salt
1½ fl oz (45 ml) lime juice
½ fl oz (15 ml) Cointreau
1½ fl oz (45 ml) tequila

1 fl oz (30 ml) blackberry liqueur
lime wedge, to garnish

GLASS
5 fl oz (145 ml) margarita glass

Rub the margarita glass rim with the lime or lemon slice and
frost with salt. Combine the liquid ingredients with ice; shake
well. Strain the drink into the glass. Garnish with the lime
wedge and serve.

serves 1

Blackcurrant Margarita

INGREDIENTS
lemon or lime slice
salt
1½ fl oz (45 ml) lime juice
½ fl oz (15 ml) Cointreau
1½ fl oz (45 ml) tequila

1 fl oz (30 ml) crème de
    cassis liqueur
lime wedge, to garnish

GLASS
7 fl oz (200 ml) cocktail glass

Rub the margarita glass rim with the lemon or lime slice and
frost with salt. Combine the liquid ingredients with ice; shake
well. Strain the drink into the glass. Garnish with the lime
wedge and serve.

serves 1

Blue Margaritas

INGREDIENTS
lime slice
salt
4 fl oz (125 ml) tequila
1 fl oz (30 ml) triple sec
2 fl oz (60 ml) lime juice
2 fl oz (60 ml) blue curaçao

1 tsp (5 ml) superfine (caster)
    sugar
lime wedges, to garnish

GLASS
5 fl oz (145 ml) margarita glass

Rub the glass rim with the lime slice and frost with salt. Half fill a cocktail shaker with ice. Add the liquid ingredients and the sugar; shake for 30 seconds. Pour into the prepared glasses with ice cubes. Garnish with a lime wedge, if you like.

serves 2

Cadillac Margarita

INGREDIENTS
lime slice
salt
1½ fl oz (45 ml) tequila
1 fl oz (30 ml) Grand Marnier

2 tsp (10 ml) lime juice
lime wedge, to garnish

GLASS
5 fl oz (145 ml) margarita glass

Rub the glass rim with the lime slice and frost with salt. Shake the tequila with the Grand Marnier and lime juice, and strain into a prepared cocktail glass. Garnish with the lime wedge.

serves 1

Catalina Margarita

INGREDIENTS
lime slice
salt
1½ fl oz (45 ml) gold tequila
1 fl oz (30 ml) peach schnapps
1 fl oz (30 ml) blue curaçao

4 fl oz (125 ml) sweet and sour
    mix (see introduction)
lime wedge, to garnish

GLASS
5 fl oz (145 ml) margarita glass

Rub the glass rim with the lime slice and frost with salt. Mix all the liquid ingredients with cracked ice in a shaker or blender and strain into the chilled prepared margarita glass. Garnish with the lime wedge.

serves 2

Chambord Margarita

INGREDIENTS
lime or lemon slice
salt
1½ fl oz (45 ml) tequila
1 fl oz (30 ml) lime or lemon
    juice
1 fl oz (30 ml) Chambord
    liqueur

½ fl oz (15 ml) Cointreau
lime wedge, to garnish

GLASS
5 fl oz (145 ml) margarita glass

Rub the glass rim with the lime or lemon slice and frost with salt. Combine the liquid ingredients with ice; shake well. Strain into the glass. Garnish with the lime wedge.

serves 1

Cherry Margarita

INGREDIENTS

lime or lemon slice
salt
1½ fl oz (45 ml) tequila
1 fl oz (30 ml) maraschino
    liqueur
1½ fl oz (45 ml) lime juice,
    freshly squeezed

½ fl oz (15 ml) Cointreau
lime slice, to garnish

GLASS

5 fl oz (145 ml) margarita glass

Rub the glass rim with lime or lemon slice and frost with salt.
Combine the liquid ingredients with ice; shake well. Strain the
drink into the glass. Garnish with the lime slice.

serves 1

Citrus Margarita

INGREDIENTS

lime or lemon slice
salt
2 fl oz (60 ml) tequila
1 fl oz (30 ml) lime juice, freshly
squeezed
1 fl oz (30 ml) orange juice,
    freshly squeezed

1 fl oz (30 ml) Cointreau
orange slice, to garnish

GLASS

7 fl oz (200 ml) cocktail glass

Rub the glass rim with the lime or lemon slice and frost with salt.
Combine the liquid ingredients with ice; shake well. Strain the
drink into the glass. Garnish with the orange slice.

serves 1

Cowboy Margaritas

INGREDIENTS
3 fl oz (90 ml) frozen limeade
    concentrate
3 fl oz (90 ml) tequila
3 fl oz (90 ml) beer

GLASS
7 fl oz (200 ml) cocktail glass

Pour the undiluted frozen limeade concentrate in a jug
(pitcher). Add the tequila and beer. Serve over plenty of ice.

serves 1

Cranberry Margarita

INGREDIENTS
lemon slice, plus extra to garnish
granulated (white) sugar
¾ fl oz (25ml) triple sec
2½ fl oz ((75 ml) cranberry juice

1½ fl oz (45 ml) tequila
¾ fl oz (25 ml) lemon juice

GLASS
7 fl oz (200 ml) cocktail glass

Rub the glass rim with the lemon slice and frost with sugar.
Combine the liquid ingredients with ice; shake well. Pour the
drink into the glass. Garnish with a lemon slice.

serves 1

Gold Margarita

INGREDIENTS
lime or lemon slice, plus extra
    to garnish
salt
½ fl oz (15 ml) Cointreau
2 fl oz (60 ml) gold tequila

1½ fl oz (45 ml) lime juice

GLASS
5 fl oz (145 ml) margarita glass

Rub the glass rim with the lime or lemon slice and frost with
salt. Combine the liquid ingredients with ice; shake well. Strain
into a glass. Garnish with the lime slice.

serves 1

Guava Margarita

INGREDIENTS
lemon slice, plus extra to garnish
sugar
¾ fl oz (25 ml) triple sec
2½ fl oz (75 ml) guava juice
1½ fl oz (45 ml) tequila

¾ fl oz (25 ml) lemon juice

GLASS
7 fl oz (200 ml) cocktail glass

Rub the glass rim with lemon slice and frost with sugar.
Combine the liquid ingredients with ice; shake well. Pour the
drink into the glass. Garnish with a lemon slice.

serves 1

Jumping Margarita

INGREDIENTS
slice of lime, plus extra to garnish
salt
½ fl oz (15 ml) lime juice
3 fl oz (90 ml) lemonade
1½ fl oz (45 ml) tequila
1 fl oz (30 ml) triple sec

1½ fl oz (45 ml) sweet-and-sour
   mix

GLASS
7 fl oz (200 ml) cocktail glass

Rub the glass rim with the lime slice and frost with salt. Mix the liquid ingredients in a shaker filled with ice; shake well. Strain into a glass. Garnish with lime slice

serves 1

Mango Margarita

INGREDIENTS
lime or lemon slice, plus extra
   to garnish
salt
1 fl oz (30 ml) lemon or lime
   juice
½ fl oz (15 ml) Cointreau

1½ fl oz (45 ml) tequila
1 fl oz (30 ml) mango liqueur

GLASS
5 fl oz (145 ml) margarita glass

Rub the glass rim with the lime or lemon slice and frost with salt. Combine the liquid ingredients with ice; shake well. Strain the drink into a glass. Garnish with a lime or lemon slice.

serves 1

Midori Margarita

INGREDIENTS

lime or lemon slice, plus extra
    to garnish
salt
1 fl oz (30 ml) Midori
2 fl oz (60 ml) tequila

1 fl oz (30 ml) lime or lemon
    juice

GLASS
5 fl oz (145 ml) margarita glass

Rub the glass rim with the lime or lemon slice and frost with
salt. Combine the liquid ingredients with ice; shake well. Strain
the drink into the glass. Garnish with a slice of lime or lemon.

serves 1

Passionfruit Margarita

INGREDIENTS

lime slice
salt
2 fl oz (60 ml) tequila
¾ fl oz (25 ml) Grand Marnier
4 fl oz (120 ml) passionfruit juice

1 lime, freshly squeezed
raspberries, to garnish

GLASS
7 fl oz (200 ml) cocktail glass

Rub the glass rim with a lime slice and frost with salt. Combine
the liquid ingredients with ice; shake well. Pour the drink into
glass over ice. Garnish with a few raspberries.

serves 1

Peach Margarita

INGREDIENTS
lime or lemon slice, plus extra
    to garnish
salt
1 fl oz (30 ml) peach liqueur
½ fl oz (15 ml) Cointreau
1½ fl oz (45 ml) tequila

1 fl oz (30 ml) lime or lemon
    juice

GLASS
5 fl oz (145 ml) margarita glass

Rub the glass rim with the lime or lemon slice and frost with
salt. Combine the liquid ingredients with ice; shake well. Strain
the drink into the glass. Garnish with a slice of lime or lemon.

serves 1

Pineapple Margarita

INGREDIENTS
lime or lemon slice
salt
2 fl oz (60 ml) tequila
2 fl oz (60 ml) pineapple juice
1 fl oz (30 ml) lime or lemon
juice, freshly squeezed

1 fl oz (30 ml) Cointreau
pineapple spear, to garnish

GLASS
7 fl oz (200 ml) cocktail glass

Rub the glass rim with the lime or lemon slice and frost with
salt. Combine the liquid ingredients with ice; shake well. Strain
the drink into the glass. Garnish with pineapple.

serves 1

MARTINI

There are many interesting stories about the origins of the martini.

• A bartender in San Francisco made up a drink for a traveller to Martinez.

• It was named for a gold miner in Martinez who struck it rich.

• It was named after the Martini and Henry rifle; the rifle was know for its 'kick'.

The Martini has added sophistication to humble gin and vodka, taking them from poor men's drinks to drinks to be enjoyed by all.

Gin was developed by a Dutch doctor (Dr Sylvius), in the 17th century, by combining alcohol with juniper berries to make a remedy for kidney complaints. This medicine has since been proved to be ineffectual, but at the time it proved to be a popular tonic that helped the patient forget their complaint, or at least dulled the pain.

William III, King of England appears to have held a grudge against the French, and raised excise on all French alcohol. This made gin, which was imported from Holland, cheaper and more accessible to the English public. The English soon started making their own, which was sold at very low prices, and for much of the 18th and early 19th centuries it became the solace of the poorer classes.

Soldiers imbibed before battle, and their drunken bravery became known as 'Dutch courage'. Juniper berries were erroneously believed to have the power to induce abortion, and thus gin also earned the name 'mother's ruin'. Living a life of debauchery earned the recipient the tag of living on 'gin lane'.

Gin has come a long way since its early days This once maligned spirit with its associations with poverty is now an intrinsic ingredient in a wide variety of distinctive cocktails.

THE PRODUCTION OF GIN

Gin is made in a continuous still from a liquid called wort. Wort is made by boiling and fermenting corn with malted barley and a small amount of another select grain. Once distilled it is then infused with other flavourings, notably juniper berries. It is almost tasteless and colourless. However some gins appear golden or straw-coloured because they have been aged in barrels. It is bottled at proofs varying from 80 to 94.

DRY GIN

Any standard gin drink ordered in your favourite bar will usually be dry gin, known as London Dry Gin. Dry gin is made using juniper berries and coriander seeds, though other flavourings are also used including almond, angelica root, cardamom, calamus root, caraway seeds, cassia, cinnamon, ginger, fennel, licorice, orris root, orange, lemon and lime peels. This collection of flavourings is known as The Botanicals.

The botanicals are added to the pot still with the neutral spirit and then redistilled, or suspended in the tower of the still allowing the spirit vapours to absorb the flavours.

Compound gin differs from distilled gin as it is made by adding the botanicals to the original distillation of the wort or by adding oils or extracts from juniper and botanicals to neutral grain spirits.

DUTCH GIN

Also known as 'Genever gin' or 'Holland's gin', Dutch gin is made by infusing juniper and some botanicals into malt wine. Malt wine is a neutral grain spirit made from equal amounts of malted barley, corn and rye. The ingredients are boiled then allowed to ferment for a few days and then distilled in a pot still. Sometimes ingredients are redistilled a few more times before again being pot stilled with the botanicals.

There are two types of Dutch gin; old (oude) and young (jonge); the younger contains much less malt wine and more continuous still grain spirit. It is not uncommon for Dutch gins to have a small amount of colouring added to the final product.

OTHER GINS

'Old Tom' is a sweet gin made in England and traditionally used to make Tom Collins cocktails.

'Plymouth gin' is completely unsweetened and is rumoured to be the traditional gin of the British navy. Generally it is the gin of preference for an authentic pink gin. Sloe gin is a mixture of dry gin and sloe berries and is the sweetest of all.

VERMOUTH

There are a number of very good vermouths available; Martini Rosso, Cinzano and Noilly-Prat are the most popular. Dry vermouth, is a clear, fortified white wine, infused, distilled or macerated with herbs, spices, caramel and other ingredients. It was developed in France early in the 19th century, and has an alcohol content of 15–18 per cent (30 to 36 proof).

Sweet vermouth originated in Italy at about the end of the 18th century, it is red/brown in colour and fairly sweet, with bitter undertones.

THE VODKATINI – THE VODKA MARTINI

Vodka has been referred to as the 'necklace of negatives' because of its distinct lack of aroma, colour and taste. It appeared in Russia int the 14th century and was referred to as *voda*, meaning water or little water (with a lot of fire).

Vodka mixes well with just about everything, be it juice, wine or other liquors and because of its negative taste it will not interfere with the flavours it is added to.

This popular spirit is made from potatoes and grain, with the most common grains used being corn, rye and wheat.

In Russia, however, vodka has been made with just about any fermenting fruit or vegetable. In Turkey it's commonly made with beets; in Britain, molasses. It is distilled at a very high alcohol content and then filtered through vegetable charcoal. To filter to a purer state, activated charcoal or very fine quartz sand is used.

MIXING MARTINIS

A martini may be shaken (James Bond style), stirred, strained, straight up, or on the rocks – it's up to you.

The original silver bullet martini had 2 fl oz (60 ml) gin and 1 fl oz (30 ml) dry vermouth.

Some martini recipes advise the use of a cocktail shaker. Another fun tool to assist your martini mixing is a pipette, to ensure just the desired amount of vermouth is infused into your cocktail.

Some people prefer a stirred martini, with a twist. To make a stirred martini, ensure that you have a good mixing glass and a muddling spoon.

GARNISHING MARTINIS

The quintessential garnish for the martini is an olive. They can be any colour and served plain or stuffed with chilli peppers and pimento. Sometimes the olive brine is also used as an ingredient, you will find this in our 'Dirty Martini'.

Of course, martinis are also garnished with lemon, lime and orange zest, slices, wedges and quarters.

MARTINI GLASSES

If a martini is your tipple of choice then why not splurge out on the best 3 fl oz (90 ml) triangle-shaped martini glasses? Martini glasses are also available in a larger 5 fl oz (150 ml) size. Remember, the better the quality of the glass, the greater the martini experience.

CHILLING THE GLASS

Martinis should be served very cold. To achieve this, run cold water over the glass, shake off the excess and place the in the refrigerator or freezer with the rim down. This allows the water to drain out and not freeze in the bottom of the glass.

Absolute Vodkatini

INGREDIENTS
1½ fl oz (45 ml) vodka
1½ tsp (7.5 ml) triple sec
½ fl oz (15 ml) fresh lemon juice
1 dash orange bitters
cocktail olives, to garnish

GLASS
3 fl oz (90 ml) martini glass

Combine the liquid ingredients with cracked ice in a cocktail shaker and shake well. Strain into a chilled martini glass and garnish with olives.

serves 1

Acetini

INGREDIENTS
1 fl oz (30 ml) gin
1½ tsp (7.5 ml) grenadine
2 tsp (10 ml) single (light) cream
½ egg white
nutmeg

GLASS
3 fl oz (90 ml) martini glass

Combine the liquid ingredients with cracked ice in a cocktail shaker and shake well. Strain into a martini glass and sprinkle with nutmeg.

serves 1

Alexandra Martini

INGREDIENTS
1 fl oz (30 ml) gin
1 fl oz (30 ml) ream
1 fl oz (30 ml) dark crème
    de cacao

GLASS
5 fl oz (150 ml) martini glass

Combine the liquid ingredients with cracked ice in a cocktail shaker and shake well. Pour slowly into a chilled cocktail glass.

serves 1

Almond Vodkatini

INGREDIENTS
1½ fl oz (45 ml) vodka
1½ tsp (7.5 ml) dry vermouth
1½ tsp (7.5 ml) Frangelico
roasted almonds, to serve

GLASS
3 fl oz (90 ml) martini glass

Combine liquid ingredients with cracked ice in a cocktail shaker and shake well. Strain into a chilled glass and serve with a few roasted almonds.

serves 1

Anglatini

INGREDIENTS
1½ fl oz (45 ml) gin
few drops grenadine cordial
2 dashes Angostura bitters
2 dashes orange bitters
olive to garnish

GLASS
3 fl oz (90 ml) martini glass

Combine liquid ingredients with cracked ice in a cocktail shaker and shake well. Strain into a chilled glass. Garnish with olives.

serves 1

Appetiser Martini

INGREDIENTS
1 fl oz (30 ml) gin
1 fl oz (30 ml) Dubonnet
cherries, to garnish

GLASS
3 fl oz (90 ml) martini glass

Combine the liquid ingredients with cracked ice in a cocktail shaker and shake well. Strain into a chilled glass and garnish with cherries.

serves 1

Berry Vodkatini

INGREDIENTS
1½ fl oz (45 ml) vodka
1½ tsp (7.5 ml) raspberry
    liqueur
fresh raspberries, to garnish

GLASS
3 fl oz (90 ml) martini glass

Combine the vodka and raspberry liqueur with cracked ice in a cocktail shaker and shake well. Strain into a chilled glass and garnish with raspberries.

serves 1

Bloody Martini

INGREDIENTS
2 fl oz (60 ml) gin
dash grenadine cordial
1½ tsp (7.5 ml) dry vermouth

GLASS
3 fl oz (90 ml) martini glass

Combine the ingredients with cracked ice in a cocktail shaker and shake well. Strain into a chilled glass.

serves 1

Blue Hawaii Martini

INGREDIENTS
1½ fl oz (45 ml) gin
1½ tsp (7.5 ml) blue curaçao
lemon twist, to garnish

GLASS
3 fl oz (90 ml) martini glass

Combine liquid ingredients in a mixing glass with ice cubes
and stir well. Strain into a chilled glass and garnish with the
lemon twist.

serves 1

Bombay Martini

INGREDIENTS
3 fl oz (90 ml) gin
splash dry vermouth
olive, to garnish

GLASS
5 fl oz (145 ml) martini glass

Combine liquid ingredients in a mixing glass with ice cubes
and stir well. Strain into a chilled glass and garnish with
the olive.

serves 1

Bostatini

INGREDIENTS
1 fl oz (30 ml) gin
1 fl oz (30 ml) apricot brandy
1 tsp (5 ml) lemon juice
1 tsp (5 ml) grenadine
black olives, to garnish

GLASS
3 fl oz (90 ml) martini glass

Combine the liquid ingredients in a mixing glass with ice cubes and stir well. Strain into a chilled glass and garnish with the black olive.

serves 1

Brekatini

INGREDIENTS
2 fl oz (60 ml) gin
splash green crème de menthe
stuffed olive, to garnish

GLASS
3 fl oz (90 ml) martini glass

Combine the liquid ingredients in a mixing glass with ice cubes and stir well. Strain into a chilled glass and garnish with the olive.

serves 1

Cajun Vodkatini

INGREDIENTS
1½ fl oz (45 ml) vodka
dash of dry vermouth
stuffed olives, to garnish

GLASS
3 fl oz (90 ml) martini glass

Combine the liquid ingredients in a mixing glass with cracked ice and stir. Strain into a chilled glass and garnish with olives.

serves 1

Campari Vodkatini

INGREDIENTS
1½ fl oz (45 ml) vodka
1½ tsp (7.5 ml) Campari
lime twist, to garnish

GLASS
3 fl oz (90 ml) martini glass

Combine the liquid ingredients with cracked ice in a cocktail shaker and shake well. Strain into a chilled glass and garnish with lime twist.

serves 1

Caprice Martini

INGREDIENTS
2 fl oz (60 ml) gin
1 fl oz (30 ml) sweet vermouth
1 fl oz (30 ml) campari

GLASS
5 fl oz (145 ml) martini glass

Combine all the ingredients with cracked ice in a cocktail shaker and shake well. Strain into a chilled martini glass.

serves 1

Caribbean Martini

INGREDIENTS
Lime slice
granulated (white) sugar
1½ fl oz (45 ml) light rum
1½ tsp (7.5 ml) dry vermouth
lime twist, to garnish

GLASS
3 fl oz (90 ml) martini glass

Run the lime slice around the rim of a chilled cocktail glass. Coat with sugar. Combine the liquid ingredients with ice in a cocktail shaker and shake well. Strain into the glass and garnish with the lime twist.

serves 1

Caribou Vodkatini

INGREDIENTS
1½ fl oz (45 ml) vodka
1½ tsp (7.5 ml) kahlúa
dry sparkling wine
lemon twist, to garnish
coffee bean, to garnish

GLASS
5 fl oz (145 ml) martini glass

Pour the vodka and kahlúa into a chilled glass. Top with sparkling wine and stir gently. Garnish with the lemon twist and drop in a coffee bean.

serves 1

Chocolate Martini

INGREDIENTS
1½ fl oz (45 ml) gin
1½ tsp (7.5 ml) Mozart
    chocolate liqueur
chocolate flakes, to garnish

GLASS
3 fl oz (90 ml) martini glass

Combine the vodka and liqueur in a mixing glass with ice and stir. Strain into a chilled glass and garnish with chocolate flakes.

serves 1

Christmas Martini

INGREDIENTS
1½ fl oz (45 ml) gin
1½ tsp (7.5 ml) vermouth
1 tsp (5 ml) peppermint
    schnapps

red and green cocktail onions,
    to garnish

GLASS
3 fl oz (90 ml) martini glass

Combine the liquid ingredients with cracked ice in a cocktail
shaker and shake well. Strain into a chilled glass and garnish
with cocktail onions.

serves 1

Citrus Martini

INGREDIENTS
1 fl oz (30 ml) gin
½ fl oz (15 ml) dry vermouth
½ fl oz (15 ml) orange juice
lemon, lime and orange wedges,
    to garnish

GLASS
3 fl oz (90 ml) martini glass

Combine the liquid ingredients with cracked ice in a cocktail
shaker and shake well. Strain into a chilled glass. Garnish with
fruit wedges.

serves 1

Citrus Vodkatini

INGREDIENTS
2 fl oz (60 ml) vodka
1 tsp (5 ml) Grand Marnier
1 tsp (5 ml) fresh lime juice
lemon wedge, to garnish

GLASS
3 fl oz (90 ml) martini glass

Combine the liquid ingredients with cracked ice in a cocktail shaker and shake well. Strain into a chilled glass and garnish with the lemon wedge.

serves 1

Cloister Martini

INGREDIENTS
2½ fl oz (75 ml) gin
2 tsp (10 ml) grapefruit juice
1 tsp (5 ml) lemon juice
1 tsp (5 ml) yellow chartreuse
lemon zest, to garnish

GLASS
3 fl oz (90 ml) martini glass

Combine all the liquid ingredients with cracked ice in a cocktail shaker and shake well. Strain into a chilled glass. Add shaved ice, if desired, and garnish with lemon zest.

serves 1

Crantini

INGREDIENTS
1½ fl oz (45 ml) gin
1½ tsp (7.5 ml) unsweetened
    cranberry juice
lime twist, to garnish

GLASS
3 fl oz (90 ml) martini glass

Pour gin into a chilled cocktail glass. Slowly add the cranberry juice. Garnish with the lime twist.

serves 1

Dirty Martini

INGREDIENTS
1½ fl oz (45 ml) gin
½ fl oz (15 ml) dry vermouth
1½ tsp (7.5 ml) olive brine
Lemon wedge

2 stuffed cocktail olives,
    to garnish

GLASS
3 fl oz (90 ml) martini glass

Combine the liquid ingredients with cracked ice in a cocktail shaker and shake well. Rub the rim of the chilled glass with a lemon wedge. Strain the liquid into the glass and garnish with two olives.

serves 1

Empire Martini

INGREDIENTS
1½ fl oz (45 ml) gin
½ fl oz (15 ml) apple brandy
½ fl oz (15 ml) apricot brandy
maraschino cherry, to garnish

GLASS
3 fl oz (90 ml) martini glass

Combine all the liquid ingredients in a mixing glass with ice
and stir well. Strain into a chilled glass and garnish with the
maraschino cherry.

serves 1

Extra Dry Vodkatini

INGREDIENTS
1½ fl oz (45 ml) vodka
5 drops dry vermouth
dash lemon juice
lemon twist, to garnish

GLASS
3 fl oz (90 ml) martini glass

Combine the liquid ingredients with cracked ice in a cocktail
shaker and shake well. Strain into a chilled glass and garnish
with the lemon twist.

serves 1

Fourth Degree

INGREDIENTS
1½ fl oz (45 ml) gin
½ fl oz (15 ml) cherry brandy
1½ tsp (7.5 ml) campari
fresh cherries, to garnish

GLASS
3 fl oz (90 ml) martini glass

Combine the liquid ingredients with cracked ice in a cocktail shaker and shake well. Strain into a chilled glass and garnish with fresh cherries.

serves 1

Gallitini

INGREDIENTS
1 fl oz (30 ml) gin
½ fl oz (15 ml) Galliano
1½ tsp (7.5 ml) sweet vermouth
1½ tsp (7.5 ml) dry vermouth
¾ fl oz (25 ml) orange juice
cocktail olive, to garnish

GLASS
5 fl oz (150 ml) martini glass

Combine the liquid ingredients in a mixing glass with cracked ice and stir well. Strain into a chilled glass and garnish with the olive.

serves 1

Gibson Martini

INGREDIENTS
2 fl oz (60 ml) gin
splash dry vermouth
2 cocktail onions, to garnish

GLASS
3 fl oz (90 ml) martini glass

Combine the liquid ingredients in a mixing glass with ice cubes and stir well. Strain into a chilled glass and garnish with the cocktail onions.

serves I

Gilded Cage Martini

INGREDIENTS
1 ½ fl oz (45 ml) gin
½ fl oz (15 ml) dry vermouth
2 dashes Angostura bitters
cocktail olive, to serve

GLASS
3 fl oz (90 ml) martini glass

Combine the liquid ingredients with cracked ice in a cocktail shaker and shake well. Strain into a chilled glass and garnish with the olive.

serves I

Gimlet Martini

INGREDIENTS
2 fl oz (60 ml) gin
½ fl oz (15 ml) lime juice
lime wedge, to garnish

GLASS
3 fl oz (90 ml) martini glass

Combine all the ingredients with cracked ice in a cocktail shaker and shake well. Strain into a chilled glass and garnish with a lime wedge.

serves 1

Gin & Sin Martini

INGREDIENTS
2 fl oz (60 ml) gin
½ fl oz (15 ml) dry vermouth

GLASS
3 fl oz (90 ml) martini glass

Combine the ingredients in the glass and serve straight up.

serves 1

Ho Ho Martini

INGREDIENTS
1 fl oz (30 ml) gin
1 fl oz (30 ml) light rum
1 ½ tsp (7.5 ml) dry vermouth
1 dash orange bitters
almond-stuffed olive, to garnish

GLASS
3 fl oz (90 ml) martini glass

Combine the liquid ingredients with cracked ice in a cocktail
shaker and shake well. Strain into a chilled glass and garnish
with the olive.

serves 1

Hot Stuff Martini

INGREDIENTS
1 ½ fl oz (45 ml) gin
½ fl oz (15 ml) dry vermouth
dash of Tabasco sauce
lime wedge, to garnish

GLASS
3 fl oz (90 ml) martini glass

Combine the liquid ingredients with cracked ice in a cocktail
shaker and shake well. Strain into a chilled glass and garnish
with the lime wedge. Add another dash or two of Tabasco, if
you like a cocktail with more bite.

serves 1

Irish Vodkatini

INGREDIENTS
Irish whiskey
1½ fl oz (45 ml) vodka
1½ tsp (7.5 ml) dry vermouth
lemon twist, to garnish

GLASS
3 fl oz (90 ml) martini glass

Rinse a chilled cocktail glass with Irish whiskey. Combine vodka and vermouth with cracked ice in a cocktail shaker and shake well. Strain into the prepared glass and garnish with the lemon twist.

serves 1

Island Martini

INGREDIENTS
1½ fl oz (45 ml) gold rum
1½ tsp (7.5 ml) dry vermouth
1½ tsp (7.5 ml) sweet vermouth
lemon twist, to garnish

GLASS
3 fl oz (90 ml) martini glass

Combine the liquid ingredients with cracked ice in a cocktail shaker and shake well. Strain into a chilled glass and garnish with the lemon twist.

serves 1

Jamaican Martini

INGREDIENTS
1½ fl oz (45 ml) gin
1½ tsp (7.5 ml) red wine
1½ tsp (7.5 ml) dark rum
5 dashes orange bitters
red chilli, to garnish

GLASS
3 fl oz (90 ml) martini glass

Combine the liquid ingredients with cracked ice in a cocktail shaker and shake well. Strain into a chilled glass and garnish with the red chilli.

serves 1

James Bond Martini

INGREDIENTS
1½ fl oz (45 ml) gin
1½ tsp (7.5 ml) vodka
1½ tsp (7.5 ml) dry vermouth
lemon twist, to garnish

GLASS
3 fl oz (90 ml) martini glass

Combine the liquid ingredients with cracked ice in a cocktail shaker and shake well. Strain into a chilled glass and garnish with the lemon twist.

serves 1

Jelly Baby Vodkatini

INGREDIENTS

lemon slice, plus extra to garnish
caster (superfine) sugar
1½ tsp (7.5 ml) dry vermouth
1 fl oz (30 ml) dark rum
1½ tsp (7.5 ml) fresh lemon
  juice
½ fl oz (15 ml) vodka
1½ tsp (7.5 ml) Southern
  Comfort
jelly babies, to garnish

GLASS

3 fl oz (90 ml) martini glass

Rub the lemon slice around the rim of a chilled cocktail glass
and frost with sugar. Combine the liquid ingredients with
cracked ice in a cocktail shaker and shake well. Strain into the
glass. Garnish with a lemon slice and jelly babies.

serves 1

Licartini

INGREDIENTS

1½ fl oz (45 ml) gin
1½ tsp (7.5 ml) Pernod
1½ tsp (7.5 ml) anisette
½ tsp (2.5 ml) orange bitters
lemon twist, to garnish

GLASS

3 fl oz (90 ml) martini glass

Combine the liquid ingredients with cracked ice in a cocktail
shaker and shake well. Pour over shaved ice into the glass and
garnish with the lemon twist.

serves 1

London Martini

INGREDIENTS
1½ fl oz (45 ml) gin
½ tsp (2.5 ml) maraschino
   liqueur
5 dashes orange bitters
½ tsp (2.5 ml) caster (superfine)
   sugar

lemon wedge, to garnish

GLASS
3 fl oz (90 ml) martini glass

Combine the liquid ingredients in a mixing glass and stir well.
Pour the mixture into a cocktail shaker with cracked ice and
sugar, then shake well. Strain into a chilled glass and garnish
with the lemon wedge.

serves 1

Manhasset

INGREDIENTS
1½ fl oz (45 ml) light rum
1½ tsp (7.5 ml) dry vermouth
1½ tsp (7.5 ml) sweet vermouth
1 tbsp (20 ml) fresh lemon juice
lemon twist, to garnish

GLASS
3 fl oz (90 ml) martini glass

Combine the liquid ingredients with cracked ice in a cocktail
shaker and shake well. Strain into a chilled glass and garnish
with the lemon twist.

serves 1

Metropolitan

INGREDIENTS
1½ fl oz (45 ml) gin
1½ tsp (7.5 ml) dry vermouth
½ fl oz (15 ml) fresh lime juice
lemon twist, to garnish

GLASS
3 fl oz (90 ml) martini glass

Combine the liquid ingredients with cracked ice in a cocktail shaker and shake well. Strain into a chilled glass and garnish with the lemon twist.

serves 1

Mexican Martini

INGREDIENTS
1½ fl oz (45 ml) gin
½ fl oz (15 ml) tequila
1½ tsp (7.5 ml) Cointreau
1 tsp (5 ml) fresh lime juice
lime wedge

GLASS
3 fl oz (90 ml) martini glass

Combine the liquid ingredients with cracked ice in a cocktail shaker and shake well. Strain into a chilled glass and garnish with lime wedge.

serves 1

Negroni

INGREDIENTS
1½ fl oz (45 ml) gin
½ fl oz (15 ml) campari
1½ tsp (7.5 ml) sweet vermouth
orange twist, to garnish

GLASS
3 fl oz (90 ml) martini glass

Combine the liquid ingredients with cracked ice in a cocktail shaker and shake well. Strain into a chilled glass and garnish with the orange twist.

serves 1

Opal Martini

INGREDIENTS
1½ fl oz (45 ml) gin
1½ tsp (7.5 ml) Cointreau
½ fl oz (15 ml) fresh orange
    juice
pinch caster (superfine) sugar

GLASS
3 fl oz (90 ml) martini glass

Combine all the ingredients with cracked ice in a cocktail shaker and shake well. Strain into a chilled glass.

serves 1

Opera Martini

INGREDIENTS
1½ fl oz (45 ml) gin
½ fl oz (15 ml) dubonnet blanc
1½ tsp (7.5 ml) maraschino
    liqueur
lemon twist, to garnish

GLASS
3 fl oz (90 ml) martini glass

Combine the liquid ingredients in a cocktail shaker with cracked ice and shake well. Strain into a chilled 3 glass and garnish with the lemon twist.

serves 1

Paisley Martini

INGREDIENTS
1½ fl oz (45 ml) gin
½ tsp (2.5 ml) dry vermouth
½ tsp (2.5 ml) Scotch whisky
cocktail olive, to garnish

GLASS
3 fl oz (90 ml) martini glass

Combine the liquid ingredients with cracked ice in a cocktail shaker and shake well. Strain into a chilled glass and garnish with the olive.

serves 1

Palm Beach Martini

INGREDIENTS
1½ fl oz (45 ml) gin
1 tsp (5 ml) sweet vermouth
1 fl oz (30 ml) grapefruit juice

GLASS
3 fl oz (90 ml) martini glass

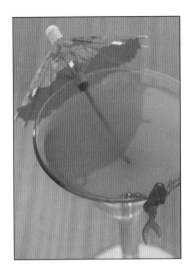

Combine all the ingredients with cracked ice in a cocktail
shaker and shake well. Strain into a chilled glass.

serves 1

Parisian Martini

INGREDIENTS
1½ fl oz (45 ml) gin
½ fl oz (15 ml) dry vermouth
1½ tsp (7.5 ml) crème de cassis
lemon twist, to garnish

GLASS
3 fl oz (90 ml) martini glass

Combine all the ingredients with cracked ice in a cocktail
shaker and shake well. Strain into a chilled glass. Garnish with
lemon twist.

serves 1

Peach Blossom Martini

INGREDIENTS
1½ fl oz (45 ml) gin
½ fl oz (15 ml) dubonnet rouge
½ fl oz (15 ml) maraschino
    liqueur
fresh peach slice, to garnish

GLASS
3 fl oz (90 ml) martini glass

Combine the liquid ingredients with cracked ice in a cocktail shaker and shake well. Strain into a chilled glass and garnish with the peach slice.

serves 1

Peppermint Vodkatini

INGREDIENTS
1½ fl oz (45 ml) vodka
½ fl oz (15 ml) white crème
    de menthe
fresh mint sprig, to garnish

GLASS
3 fl oz (90 ml) martini glass

Combine the liquid ingredients with cracked ice in a cocktail shaker and shake well. Strain into a chilled glass and garnish with the mint sprig.

serves 1

Perfecto Martini

INGREDIENTS
1½ fl oz (45 ml) gin
1½ tsp (7.5 ml) dry vermouth
1½ tsp (7.5 ml) sweet vermouth
cocktail olive, to garnish

GLASS
3 fl oz (90 ml) martini glass

Combine the liquid ingredients with cracked ice in a cocktail shaker and shake well. Strain into a chilled glass and garnish with the olive.

serves 1

Portini

INGREDIENTS
1½ fl oz (45 ml) gin
1½ tsp (7.5 ml) ruby port
2 tsp (10 ml) fresh lime juice
1 tsp (5 ml) grenadine
lime twist, to serve

GLASS
3 fl oz (90 ml) martini glass

Combine the liquid ingredients with cracked ice in a cocktail shaker and shake well. Strain into a chilled glass and garnish with the lime twist.

serves 1

Road Runner Vodkatini

INGREDIENTS
1½ fl oz (45 ml) vodka
1½ tsp (7.5 ml) dry vermouth
1½ tsp (7.5 ml) gold tequila
jalapeno-stuffed olive, to garnish

GLASS
3 fl oz (90 ml) martini glass

Combine the liquid ingredients with cracked ice in a cocktail shaker and shake well. Strain into a chilled glass and garnish with the stuffed olive.

serves 1

Russatini

INGREDIENTS
1½ fl oz (45 ml) gin
½ fl oz (15 ml) vodka
red cherry, to garnish

GLASS
3 fl oz (90 ml) martini glass

Combine the liquid ingredients with cracked ice in a cocktail shaker and shake well. Strain into a chilled glass and garnish with a red cherry.

serves 1

Seventh Heaven Martini

INGREDIENTS
1½ fl oz (45 ml) gin
1½ tsp (7.5 ml) maraschino
   liqueur
1½ tsp (7.5 ml) grapefruit juice
fresh mint sprig, to garnish

GLASS
3 fl oz (90 ml) martini glass

Combine the liquid ingredients with cracked ice in a cocktail
shaker and shake well. Strain into the chilled glass and garnish
with the mint sprig.

serves 1

Silver Bullet Martini

INGREDIENTS
1½ fl oz (45 ml) gin
1½ tsp (7.5 ml) dry vermouth
cocktail olive

GLASS
3 fl oz (90 ml) martini glass

Combine the liquid ingredients in a mixing glass with ice cubes
and stir well. Strain into a chilled glass and garnish with olive.

serves 1

Silver Streak Martini

INGREDIENTS
1½ fl oz (45 ml) gin
¾ fl oz (25 ml) Jägermeister
lemon twist, to garnish

GLASS
3 fl oz (90 ml) martini glass

Combine the liquid ingredients with cracked ice in a cocktail shaker and shake well. Strain into a chilled glass and garnish with the lemon twist.

serves 1

Sweet & Spicy Martini

INGREDIENTS
1½ fl oz (45 ml) gin
1½ tsp (7.5 ml) sweet vermouth
1½ tsp (7.5 ml) orange liqueur
cinnamon stick, to garnish

GLASS
3 fl oz (90 ml) martini glass

Combine the liquid ingredients with cracked ice in a cocktail shaker and shake well. Strain into a chilled glass and garnish with the cinnamon stick.

serves 1

Tequini

INGREDIENTS
1½ fl oz (45 ml) silver tequila
1½ tsp (7.5 ml) dry vermouth
1 dash orange bitters
lemon twist, to garnish

GLASS
3 fl oz (90 ml) martini glass

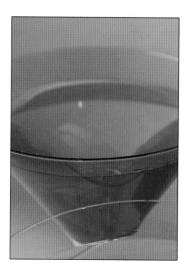

Combine the liquid ingredients with cracked ice in a cocktail shaker and shake well. Strain into a chilled glass and garnish with the lemon twist. Enhance this cocktail by rubbing a lemon slice over the rim of the glass, if you like.

serves 1

Untied Vodkatini

INGREDIENTS
1½ fl oz (45 ml) vodka
1½ fl oz (45 ml) Galliano
1½ tsp (7.5 ml) grenadine
    cordial
large lemon slice, to garnish

GLASS
3 fl oz (90 ml) martini glass

Combine liquid ingredients in a mixing glass with cracked ice and stir well. Strain into a chilled glass and garnish with the large lemon slice.

serves 1

Shooters

Shooters contain mixed shots of liquor and can include non-alcoholic drinks that total 1 fl oz (30 ml). They can be shaken, stirred, mixed or served straight up. Bartenders often have their own signature shooter and many give them fancy names. These drinks are intended to be drunk quickly with one tip of the glass, rather than sipped, so that you get one potent flavour hit. Like shots, they are served in shot glasses.

Backfire

INGREDIENTS
2 tsp (10 ml) kahlúa
2 tsp (10 ml) Baileys
2 tsp (10 ml) vodka

Layer the ingredients in the order given from top to bottom in a shot glass. Serve straight up.

serves 1

GLASS
1½ fl oz (45 ml) shot glass

Baileys Dream

INGREDIENTS
1 tsp (5 ml) kahlúa
1 tsp (5 ml) white crème de
   cacao
2 tsp (10 ml) Tia Maria
1 tsp (5 ml) Baileys

Layer the ingredients in the order given into a shot glass. Serve straight up.

serves 1

GLASS
1½ fl oz (45 ml) shot glass

Brain Haemorrhage

INGREDIENTS

1 fl oz (30 ml) peach schnapps
1 tsp (5 ml) Baileys
3 dashes grenadine coridal

GLASS

1½ fl oz (45 ml) shot glass

Pour each drink in order into the glass, allowing each to settle before carefully adding the next. Do not stir.

serves 1

Chocolate Chimp

INGREDIENTS

½ fl oz (15 ml) dark crème
  de cacao
½ fl oz (15 ml) Tia Maria
½ fl oz (15 ml) banana liqueur

GLASS

Tall cordial glass

Layer the ingredients in the order given in a cordial glass.

serves 1

Christmas Tree

INGREDIENTS
½ fl oz (15 ml) vodka
½ fl oz (15 ml) green crème de
    menthe
½ fl oz (15 ml) cherry brandy

Layer the ingredients in the order given into a tall cordial glas.

serves 1

GLASS
Tall cordial glass

Estonian Forest Fire

INGREDIENTS
1 fl oz (30 ml) vodka
12 drops Tabasco Sauce
1 kiwi, to garnish

Pour the vodka and Tabasco into a shot glass. Stir and serve with a kiwi fruit, which should be eaten after the shot has been consumed.

GLASS
1 ½ fl oz (45 ml) shot glass

E.T.

INGREDIENTS

2 tsp (10 ml) Midori
2 tsp (10 ml) Baileys
2 tsp (10 ml) vodka

GLASS

1½ fl oz (45 ml) shot glass

Layer the ingredients in a shot glass working from top to bottom of the ingredient's list. Allow each to settle before adding the next.

serves 1

Fifth Avenue

INGREDIENTS

½ fl oz (15 ml) dark crème de cacao
½ fl oz (15 ml) apricot brandy
½ fl oz (15 ml) single (light) cream (chilled)

GLASS

Tall cordial glass

Layer the ingredients in a shot glass working from top to bottom of the ingredient's list. Allow each to settle before adding the next.

serves 1

Golden Flash

INGREDIENTS
2 tsp (10 ml) amaretto
2 tsp (10 ml) triple sec
2 tsp (10 ml) sambuca

GLASS
1½ fl oz (45 ml) shot glass

Layer the ingredients in a shot glass working from top to bottom of the ingredient's list. Allow each to settle before adding the next.

serves 1

Green Apple

INGREDIENTS
1 fl oz (30 ml) Southern
  Comfort
1 tsp (5 ml) Midori
1 tsp (5 ml) sweet and sour mix

GLASS
1½ fl oz (45 ml) shot glass

Pour all the ingredients into a mixing glass over ice and stir. Strain into a chilled shot glass.

serves 1

G-Spot

INGREDIENTS
½ fl oz (15 ml) chambord
½ fl oz (15 ml) southern
   comfort
½ fl oz (15 ml) fresh orange
   juice

GLASS
1½ fl oz (45 ml) shot glass

Pour the ingredients into a cocktail shaker over ice and shake.
Strain into a chilled glass.

serves 1

Jellyfish

INGREDIENTS
½ fl oz (15 ml) amaretto
½ fl oz (15 ml) dark crème de
   cacao
1½ tsp (7.5 ml) Baileys
3 drops grenadine

GLASS
1½ fl oz (45 ml) shot glass

Pour the amaretto and cacao into a shot glass allowing the
amaretto to settle before adding the cacao. Carefully add the
Baileys and then add the grenadine.

serves 1

Hard Rock

INGREDIENTS
2 tsp (10 ml) Midori
2 tsp (10 ml) vodka
2 tsp (10 ml) Baileys

GLASS
1½ fl oz (45 ml) shot glass

Layer the ingredients in order in the glass and serve.

serves 1

Hiroshima Bomber

INGREDIENTS
¾ fl oz (22 ml) triple sec
1½ tsp (7.5 ml) Baileys
3 drops grenadine

GLASS
1½ fl oz (45 ml) shot glass

Pour the triple sec into the glass and layer the Baileys on top. Drop the grenadine into the centre of the liquid.

serves 1

King's Cup

INGREDIENTS
½ fl oz (15 ml) Galliano
1 ½ tsp (7.5 ml) double (heavy)
cream

GLASS
1 ½ fl oz (45 ml) shot glass

Layer the ingredients in the order given. Serve straight up.

serves 1

Lava Lamp

INGREDIENTS
1 ½ tsp (7.5 ml) kahlúa
1 ½ tsp (7.5 ml) strawberry
liqueur
1 ½ tsp (7.5 ml) Frangelico
1 ½ tsp (7.5 ml) Baileys

3 drops advocaat

GLASS
1 ½ fl oz (45 ml) shot glass

Pour the kahlúa, strawberry liqueur and Frangelico into a shot glass but do not stir. Allow to settle. Layer the Baileys on top. Drop in the advocaat.

serves 1

Mexican Chicken

INGREDIENTS
1 fresh egg
1 fl oz (30 ml) tequila
Dash Tabasco sauce

GLASS
1½ fl oz (45 ml) shot glass

Crack the egg into a liqueur glass and add the tequila. Add the sauce and serve.

serves 1

Okanagan

INGREDIENTS
2 tsp (10 ml) blue curaçao
½ fl oz (15 ml) strawberry
   liqueur
1 tsp (5 ml) coconut liqueur

GLASS
1½ fl oz (45 ml) shot glass

Layer the ingredients in order allowing each to settle before adding the next. Serve straight up.

serves 1

Placenta

INGREDIENTS
½ fl oz (15 ml) amaretto
½ fl oz (15 ml) Baileys
3 drops grenadine

GLASS
Shot glass

Pour the amaretto and Baileys to the shot glass, but do not stir. Drop in the grenadine.

serves 1

Rare Velvet

INGREDIENTS
2 tsp (10 ml) dark crème
   de cacao
2 tsp (10 ml) green crème
   de menthe
2 tsp (10 ml) brandy

GLASS
Shot glass

Layer the cacao, crème de menthe and brandy into the glass.

serves 1

Smurf Town

INGREDIENTS
½ fl oz (15 ml) blue curaçao
½ fl oz (15 ml) peach schnapps
Fresh whipped cream, to serve
5 drops grenadine

GLASS
Shot glass

Pour the curaçao and schnapps into a shot glass. Float a small spoonful of cream on top. Drop the grenadine on the cream.

serves 1

The Girl Mom Warned You About

INGREDIENTS
1 ½ tsp (7.5 ml) grenadine
1 ½ tsp (7.5 ml) triple sec
1 ½ tsp (7.5 ml) light rum
1 ½ tsp (7.5 ml) Midori
1 ½ tsp (7.5 ml) blue curaçao

GLASS
Shot glass

Layer the ingredients in order. Serve straight up.

serves 1

Warm Leatherette

INGREDIENTS
½ fl oz (15 ml) black sambuca
2 tsp (10 ml) amaretto
1 tsp (5 ml) grenadine

GLASS
Cordial glass

Pour the sambuca into the glass and layer the amaretto on top. Pour the grenadine down the inside of the glass and allow to settle at the base of the drink.

serves 1

Water–Bubba

INGREDIENTS
½ fl oz (15 ml) cherry advocaat
2 tsp (10 ml) advocaat
2½ tsp (12.5 ml) blue curaçao

GLASS
Cordial glass

Layer the ingredients in the order given and serve straight up.

serves 1

Crème–based Drinks

Many people who are not easily enticed by a whisky sour or a Long Island iced tea prefer a friendlier, more gentle drink. Be warned though, many of these are very drinkable, smooth and creamy drinks. They contain potent combinations, regardless of how delicious they seem or how easily they go down. Enjoy.

Alexander

INGREDIENTS
1 fl oz (30 ml) gin
1 fl oz (30 ml) white crème de
    cacao
1 fl oz (30 ml) heavy (double)
    cream
ground (powdered) nutmeg

GLASS
5 fl oz (145 ml) cocktail glass

Shake all the liquid ingredients with ice and strain into a
cocktail glass. Sprinkle nutmeg on top.

serves 1

Almond Joy

INGREDIENTS
½ fl oz (15 ml) amaretto
½ fl oz (15 ml) white crème
    de cacao
2 fl oz (60 ml) heavy (double)
    cream
1 cherry, to garnish

GLASS
5 fl oz (145 ml) cocktail glass

Blend all the liquid ingredients with ice and strain into the
glass. Garnish with the cherry.

serves 1

Banshee

INGREDIENTS
½ fl oz (15 ml) banana liqueur
½ fl oz (15 ml) white crème
    de cacao
2 fl oz (60 ml) heavy (double)
    cream

GLASS
5 fl oz (145 ml) cocktail glass

Blend all the ingredients with ice and strain into the glass.

serves 1

Bright Eyes

INGREDIENTS
1 fl oz (30 ml) white crème
    de cacao
1 fl oz (30 ml) strawberry
    liqueur
1 fl oz (30 ml) vodka
1 fl oz (30 ml) heavy (double)
    cream

1 fl oz (30 ml) banana liqueur
6 ripe strawberries
chocolate flakes, to garnish

GLASS
8 fl oz (230 ml) martini glass

Blend all the liquid ingredients with five strawberries and ice, then pour into the glass. Garnish with the remaining strawberry and sprinkle chocolate flakes on top.

serves 1

Calcutta Flip

INGREDIENTS
1½ fl oz (45 ml) dark rum
1½ fl oz (45 ml) light (single)
   cream
¾ fl oz (22 ml) sugar syrup
   (see introduction)
2 tsp (10 ml) orange-flavoured
   liqueur

1 egg yolk
ground (powdered) nutmeg

GLASS
5 fl oz (145 ml) cocktail glass

Shake all ingredients except for the nutmeg with ice and strain
into the glass. Sprinkle the nutmeg on top.

serves 1

Cantaloupe Dream

INGREDIENTS
1 fl oz (30 ml) maraschino
   liqueur
1 fl oz (30 ml) Galliano
1 fl oz (30 ml) orange juice
1 fl oz (30 ml) heavy (double)
   cream

3 scoops fresh rock melon, plus
   1 rock melon ball
sprig of fresh mint

GLASS
10 fl oz (285 ml) hi-ball glass

Blend all the liquid ingredients and the three scoops of rock
melon with ice and strain into a glass. Garnish with the rock
melon balls on the side of the glass with the mint.

serves 1

Climax

INGREDIENTS

½ fl oz (15 ml) amaretto
½ fl oz (15 ml) white crème
    de cacao
½ fl oz (15 ml) Cointreau
½ fl oz (15 ml) banana liqueur
½ fl oz (15 ml) vodka

2 fl oz (30 ml) double (heavy)
    cream

GLASS

5 fl oz (145 ml) cocktail glass

Blend all ingredients with ice and strain into cocktail glass.

serves 1

Godson

INGREDIENTS

1 fl oz (30 ml) Galliano
1 fl oz (30 ml) amaretto
1 fl oz (30 ml) heavy (double)
    cream
ground (powdered) cinnamon

GLASS

7 fl oz (200 ml) old-fashioned
    glass

Build the liquid over ice cubes in the glass and stir. Sprinkle with cinnamon.

serves 1

Gumbo Fizz

INGREDIENTS

2 fl oz (60 ml) gin
1 fl oz (30 ml) lemon juice
1 fl oz (30 ml) heavy (double)
   cream
1 tsp (5 ml) superfine (caster)
   sugar

1 egg white
1 tsp (5 ml) Cointreau
3 fl oz (90 ml) soda water

GLASS

10 fl oz (285 ml) hi-ball glass

Shake all the ingredients except the soda water with ice and
strain into a glass almost filled with ice cubes. Add the soda
water and stir well.

serves 1

Love in the Afternoon

INGREDIENTS

1 fl oz (30 ml) dark rum
1 fl oz (30 ml) orange juice
1 fl oz (30 ml) coconut cream
½ fl oz (15 ml) heavy (double)
   cream
½ fl oz (15 ml) sugar syrup (see
   introduction)

6 ripe strawberries
chocolate flakes

GLASS

5 fl oz (145 ml) Champagne
   saucer

Blend all liquid ingredients with five of the strawberries and
ice, then pour into the glass. Garnish with the remaining
strawberry and sprinkle chocolate flakes on top.

serves 1

Matinée

INGREDIENTS
2 fl oz (60 ml) gin
1 fl oz (30 ml) sambuca clear
1 egg white
4 dashes of lime juice
1 fl oz (30 ml) heavy (double)
    cream

ground (powdered) nutmeg

GLASS
5 fl oz (145 ml) martini glass

Shake all the ingredients except nutmeg with ice and strain into the martini glass. Sprinkle nutmeg on top.

serves 1

Multiple Orgasm

INGREDIENTS
1 fl oz (30 ml) Baileys
1 fl oz (30 ml) Cointreau
1 fl oz (30 ml) heavy (double)
    cream
1 red cherry
ground (powdered) cinnamon

GLASS
7 fl oz (200 ml) cocktail glass

Build the liquid over ice cubes in the glass and stir. Garnish with the cherry and cinnamon.

serves 1

Pink Poodle

INGREDIENTS
1 fl oz (30 ml) campari
1 fl oz (30 ml) dry gin
1½ fl oz (30 ml) double (heavy)
    cream
4 strawberries

GLASS
145 ml (5 fl oz) Champagne
    saucer

Blend all the ingredients with ice and pour into the glass.

serves 1

Pink Squirrel

INGREDIENTS
½ fl oz (15 ml) crème de
    almond
½ fl oz (15 ml) white crème
    de cacao

60 ml (2 fl oz) double (heavy)
    cream

GLASS
145 ml (5 fl oz) cocktail glass

Blend all ingredients with ice and strain into the cocktail glass.

serves 1

Silk Stockings

INGREDIENTS
1 fl oz (30 ml) tequila
1 fl oz (30 ml) white crème
   de menthe
dash of grenadine
1 fl oz (30 ml) double (heavy)
   cream

1 red cherry, to garnish
ground (powdered) cinnamon,
   to sprinkle

GLASS
5 fl oz (145 ml) Champagne
   saucer

Blend all the liquid ingredients with ice and strain into a
Champagne saucer. Garnish with a red cherry and sprinkle
cinnamon on top.

serves 1

Sombrero

INGREDIENTS
1½ fl oz (45 ml) coffee liqueur
30 ml double (heavy) cream

GLASS
17½ fl oz (650 ml) brandy
   balloon

Shake all the ingredients with ice and strain into a chilled
brandy balloon.

serves 1

Strawberry Tremor

INGREDIENTS

1 fl oz (30 ml) strawberry
   liqueur
½ fl oz (15 ml) white crème
   de cacao
2 fl oz (60 ml) double (heavy)
   cream

4 strawberries

GLASS

5 fl oz (145 ml) Champagne
   saucer

Blend the liquid ingredients with 3 strawberries and ice and
pour into a Champagne saucer. Garnish with the remaining
strawberry on the side of the glass.

serves 1

Sweet Lady Jane

INGREDIENTS

½ fl oz (15 ml) white curaçao
1 fl oz (30 ml) strawberry
   liqueur
1 fl oz (30 ml) double (heavy)
   cream
½ fl oz (15 ml) orange juice

½ fl oz (15 ml) coconut cream
1 strawberry, to garnish
chocolate flakes, to sprinkle

GLASS

5 fl oz (145 ml) Champagne
   saucer

Shake all liquid ingredients with ice and strain into the
Champagne saucer. Garnish with a strawberry on the side of
the glass and sprinkle chocolate flakes on top.

serves 1

White Heart

INGREDIENTS
½ fl oz (15 ml) sambuca clear
½ fl oz (15 ml) white crème
   de cacao
2 fl oz (60 ml) double (heavy)
   cream

GLASS
5 fl oz (145 ml) cocktail glass

Blend all the ingredients with ice and pour into the cocktail glass. Serve with a straw and stirrer.

serves 1

White Russian

INGREDIENTS
2 fl oz (60 ml) vodka
1 fl oz (30 ml) white crème
   de cacao
1 fl oz (30 ml) double (heavy)
   cream

GLASS
5 fl oz (145 ml) cocktail glass

Shake all the ingredients with ice and strain into the cocktail glass.

serves 1

Frozen Drinks

Frozen drinks are the fast way to cool down the crowd on a balmy day, making your guests relaxed and chilled at the same time. Take the heat out of the party and the sting out of a busy day with cool cleansing offerings that can be sipped slowly and still remain quenching as they melt away. Fresh fruits are the key here – when you include seasonal fruit in these cocktails they will have an unmistakable extra dimension.

Banana Daiquiri

INGREDIENTS

1½ fl oz (45 ml) light rum
½ fl oz (15 ml) Cointreau
1½ fl oz (45 ml) lime juice
1 tsp (5 ml) sugar
1 medium banana, sliced

lemon twist, to garnish

GLASS

5 fl oz (145 ml) Champagne
flute

Blend all the ingredients except the lemon with ½ cup crushed ice until smooth, then pour into a Champagne flute. Garnish with a lemon twist.

serves 1

Blushin' Russian

INGREDIENTS

1 fl oz (30 ml) coffee liqueur
1 fl oz (30 ml) vodka
1 scoop vanilla ice cream
4 large strawberries

GLASS

5 fl oz (145 ml) Champagne
flute

Blend all the ingredients except 1 strawberry with ½ cup crushed ice until smooth. Pour into a Champagne flute. Serve with a straw and garnish with the remaining strawberry.

serves 1

Devil's Tail

INGREDIENTS
1½ fl oz (45 ml) light rum
1 fl oz (30 ml) vodka
1½ tsp (7.5 ml) grenadine
1½ tsp (7.5 ml) apricot brandy
wedge of lime, to garnish

GLASS
5 fl oz (145 ml) Champagne
  flute

Blend all liquid ingredients with ½ cup crushed ice until smooth. Pour into a Champagne flute. Serve with a straw and garnish with a lime wedge.

serves 1

Frozen Blue Margarita

INGREDIENTS
wedge of lime
salt
4 fl oz (120 ml) tequila
1 fl oz (30 ml) Cointreau
2 fl oz (60 ml) lime juice
2 fl oz (60 ml) blue curaçao

1 tsp (5 ml) caster (superfine)
  sugar

GLASS
12 fl oz (350 ml) margarita glass

Rub the edge of the margarita glass with the lime wedge and frost with salt. Mix all the remaining ingredients in a blender with ice until slushy. Pour into the prepared glass.

serves 1

Frozen Cherry Margarita

INGREDIENTS
wedge of lime
salt
6 maraschino cherries
1½ fl oz (45 ml) tequila
1 fl oz (30 ml) lime juice

1 fl oz (30 ml) maraschino
   liqueur

GLASS
12 fl oz (350 ml) margarita glass

Rub the glass rim with the lime wedge and frost with salt. In a blender, combine the maraschino cherries with the liquids. Blend until smooth. With the motor running, add ice cubes a few at a time until the mixture becomes thick and slushy. Pour into the glass.

serves 1

Frozen Daiquiri

INGREDIENTS
1½ fl oz (45 ml) light rum
½ fl oz (15 ml Cointreau
1½ fl oz (45 ml) lime juice
1 tsp (5 ml) sugar
1 cherry, to garnish

GLASS
5 fl oz (145 ml) cocktail glass

Blend all of the ingredients except the cherry with ½ cup crushed ice until smooth, then pour into the cocktail glass. Garnish with the cherry.

serves 1

Frozen Double Apricot Margarita

INGREDIENTS

lime or lemon slices, plus extra
  to garnish
coarse salt
1¼ cups fresh apricots halved,
  pitted unpeeled or
  1 lb (450 g) canned apricot
  halves (drained)
2 fl oz (55 ml) tequila

2 oz (55 g) granulated (white)
  sugar
2 fl oz (55 ml) lime juice
2 fl oz (55 ml) apricot nectar
3 cups ice cubes
extra lime juice

GLASS

12 fl oz (350 ml) margarita glass

Rub the margarita glass rims with a lime or lemon slice and frost
with salt. In a blender, combine the apricot halves, tequila, sugar,
lime juice and apricot nectar. Blend until smooth. Add the ice cubes
a few at a time until the mixture becomes thick and slushy. Pour
into prepared glasses. Garnish with lime or lemon slice.

serves 2–4

Frozen Italian Margarita

INGREDIENTS
lime or lemon slices, plus extra
   for garnishing
salt
6 fl oz (180 ml) frozen lemonade
   concentrate

3 fl oz (90 ml) tequila
2 fl oz (60 ml) amaretto
1 fl oz (30 ml) Cointreau

GLASS
12 fl oz (350 ml) margarita glass

Rub the margarita glass rim with a lime or lemon slice and
frost with salt. Put all liquid ingredients and 1 cup ice in a
blender and blend until slushy. Pour into the glass, garnish with
the remaining lime or lemon slice.

serves 1

Frozen Kiwi Margarita

INGREDIENTS
3 wedges of lime
salt
4 fl oz (120 ml) silver tequila
4 fl oz (120 ml) triple sec
8 fl oz (250 ml) lemon juice
4 fl oz (120 ml) lime juice

3½ oz (90 g) caster (superfine)
   sugar
2 kiwi fruit, peeled

GLASS
12 fl oz (350 ml) margarita glass

Rub the margarita glass rims with 1 wedge of lime and
frost with salt. Put the liquid ingredients, sugar and kiwi fruit
into a blender, then add the ice. Blend until slushy, pour into
the margarita glasses. Farnish with the remaining lime wedges.

serves 2

Frozen Lavender Margaritas

INGREDIENTS
20 ml (1 tbsp) sugar
1 tsp (5 ml) fresh lavender
wedge of lime
8 fl oz (250 ml) tequila
4 fl oz (120 ml) blue curaçao
8 fl oz (250 ml) coconut milk

3 fl oz (90 ml) lime juice
450 g (1 lb) frozen raspberries
450 g (1 lb) frozen blueberries
lavender sprigs, rinsed, to garnish

GLASS
12 fl oz (350 ml) margarita glass

Mash the sugar and lavender in a saucer to release the flavour. Rub the glass rims with lime, then frost with the lavender sugar. In a blender, combine the liquids. Gradually add the fruit. Top up with ice. Blend until smooth and slushy. Pour into glasses. Garnish with lavender sprigs.

serves 8–10

Frozen Mango Margarita

INGREDIENTS
wedge of lime
sugar
1½ fl oz (45 ml) silver tequila
1 fl oz (30 ml) triple sec
1½ fl oz (45 ml) lemon juice,
    freshly squeezed

2 fl oz (60 ml) sweet-and-sour
    mix (see introduction)
¾ cup mango, partially frozen
1 mango slice, to garnish

GLASS
1½ cups (12 fl oz/340 ml)
margarita glass

Rub the rim of the glass with the lime wedge and frost with sugar. Mix the liquids with frozen mango and ice in a blender and blend until slushy. Pour into the glass. Garnish with mango.

serves 1

Frozen Matador

INGREDIENTS
slice of lime
salt
1½ fl oz (45 ml) tequila
2 fl oz (60 ml) pineapple juice
4 tsp (20 ml) lime juice

1 pineapple spear

GLASS
6 fl oz (170 ml) old-fashioned
  glass

Rub the rim of the glass with lime and frost with salt. Blend the liquid ingredients with 1 cup of crushed ice until smooth. Pour into the glass. Serve with a straw and garnish with the pineapple spear.

serves 1

Frozen Papaya Margarita

INGREDIENTS
slice of lime
salt
1 papaya, chopped
4 fl oz (125 ml) gold tequila
2½ fl oz (75 ml) Cointreau

2 fl oz (60 ml) lime juice

GLASS
12 fl oz (340 ml) margarita glass

Rub the rim of the glass with lime and frost with salt. Purée the papaya until smooth and refrigerate for 1 hour. Add the tequila, Cointreau, lime juice and 1 cup of crushed ice. Blend on high until thick and slushy. Pour into the prepared glass.

serves 1

Frozen Strawberry Margaritas

INGREDIENTS
2¼ lb (1 kg) seedless
    watermelon, cut into
    25 mm (1 in) chunks
1 lime, cut into wedges
salt
6 fl oz (180 ml) tequila

4 fl oz (120 ml) Cointreau
2½ fl oz (75 ml) fresh lime juice

GLASS
12 fl oz (340 ml) margarita glass

Freeze the melon chunks in a plastic bag until solid. Rub the margarita glass rims with a lime wedge and frost with salt. Blend the liquids and watermelon until fairly smooth. Divide the mixture among the glasses. Squeeze a lime wedge into each cocktail, drop the wedge into the glass.

serves 4

Frozen Watermelon Margaritas

INGREDIENTS
1 lime or lemon, cut into slices
salt
6 fl oz (180 ml) tequila
2 fl oz (60 ml) Cointreau
2 fl oz (60 ml) frozen limeade
    concentrate

1 cup frozen strawberries

GLASS
12 fl oz (340 ml) margarita glass

Rub the glass rims with lime or lemon slices and frost with salt. Combine the liquid ingredients, strawberries and 8 cups ice in a blender and process until slushy. Pour into the prepared glasses, and garnish with lime or lemon slices.

serves 4

Frozen Margaritas with Lime

INGREDIENTS

1 lime, cut into slices
sugar
13 fl oz (380 ml) sweet-and-sour
    mix (see introduction)
4 fl oz (120 ml) tequila
2½ fl oz (75 ml) papaya nectar

2½ fl oz (75 ml) guava nectar
2 fl oz (60 ml) coconut cream

GLASS
12 fl oz (340 ml) margarita glass

Rub 6 glass rims with lime slices and frost with sugar.
Combine the remaining ingredients in a blender with 8 ice
cubes and process until well blended. Pour into the glasses
and garnish each with slices of lime.

serves 6

Gulfstream

INGREDIENTS

slice of orange
sugar
1 fl oz (30 ml) blue curaçao
3 fl oz (90 ml) Champagne
½ fl oz (15 ml) light rum
½ fl oz (15 ml) brandy

6 fl oz (180 ml) lemonade
1 fl oz (30 ml) lime juice
1 strawberry, halved

GLASS
7 fl oz (200 ml) footed tulip

Rub the rim of each glass with orange and frost with sugar.
Blend the liquid ingredients with 1 cup of crushed ice until
smooth. Pour into glasses and garnish with the strawberry.

serves 2

Mexican Runner

INGREDIENTS
1 fl oz (30 ml) tequila
1 fl oz (30 ml) lime juice
½ fl oz (15 ml) Tia Maria
½ fl oz (15 ml) Grand Marnier
half a banana
½ fl oz (15 ml) blackberry
    liqueur

2 strawberries, 1 to garnish
cocktail umbrella, to decorate

GLASS
10 fl oz (285 ml) cocktail glass

Blend all ingredients except for the garnish and pour into the cocktail glass. Garnish with the strawberry and umbrella.

serves 1

Honeydew Margaritas

INGREDIENTS
lime slice
salt
3 cups diced ripe honeydew
    melon
2 fl oz (55 ml) gold tequila
2 fl oz (55 ml) triple sec

2 fl oz (55 ml) lime juice
14 ice cubes
6 lime wedges, to garnish

GLASS
7 fl oz (200 ml) footed tulip

Rub the glass rims with the lime slice and frost with salt. Blend the melon and liquids with the ice cubes until slushy. Pour into prepared glasses, then garnish each with a lime wedge.

serves 2–4

Yucatan Margaritas with Tropical Fruit

INGREDIENTS

12 lime wedges
6 fl oz (175 ml) papaya nectar
1½ oz (40 g) granulated (white)
  sugar
6 fl oz (175 ml) guava nectar
1¼ pints (750 ml) sweet-and-
  sour mix

4 fl oz (120 ml) canned cream
  of coconut
16 ice cubes
1 cup tequila
12 lime slices, to garnish

GLASS

7 fl oz (200 ml) footed tulip

Rub the glass rims with lime wedge and frost with sugar.
Combine half of the remaining ingredients (except lime slices)
in a blender. Process until well blended. Pour into 6 glasses.
Repeat with remaining half of the ingredients. Garnish each
glass with a lime slice.

serves 12

Hot Drinks

The winter warmers collection are drinks to soothe and comfort you. Nothing pleases more than a warming drink that heats you up from the inside out and relaxes you at the same time. This chapter contains appealing drinks for bitterly cold night when a treat is required. With a bit of planning, you can pack some equipment and be the toast of the ski lodge or chalet.

Baileys Irish Coffee

INGREDIENTS
1 fl oz (30 ml) Baileys
1 tsp (5 ml) brown sugar
hot coffee
whipped cream
chocolate flakes, to decorate

GLASS
7½ fl oz (230 ml) Irish coffee
glass

Pour Baileys into the glass and stir in the brown sugar. Fill to within ½ in (15 mm) of top with hot coffee. Cover with whipped cream, then top with chocolate flakes.

serves 1

Bedroom Farce

INGREDIENTS
1 fl oz (30 ml) dark rum
½ fl oz 15 ml Bourbon
2 tsp (10 ml) Galliano
4 fl oz (120 ml) hot chocolate
2 fl oz (60 ml) double (heavy)
cream

½ tsp (2.5 ml) grated (shredded)
dark (bittersweet) chocolate

GLASS
7½ fl oz (230 ml) Irish coffee
glass

Pour first three ingredients into an Irish coffee glass, then add hot chocolate. Carefully spoon cream on top, and sprinkle with the grated chocolate.

serves 1

Black Gold

INGREDIENTS
4 fl oz (120 ml) black coffee
½ fl oz (15 ml) Cointreau
½ fl oz (15 ml) amaretto
½ fl oz (15 ml) Baileys
½ fl oz (15 ml) Frangelico
whipped cream

chocolate flakes, to decorate
ground (powdered) cinnamon,
   to decorate

GLASS
7½ fl oz (230 ml) Irish coffee
   glass

Pour the first five ingredients into the glass, and stir well.
Carefully spoon cream on top, then sprinkle with chocolate
flakes and ground cinnamon.

serves 1

Black Stripe

INGREDIENTS
2 fl oz (60 ml) dark rum
4 tsp (20 ml) molasses
1 tsp (5 ml) honey
lemon twist, to garnish

GLASS
7½ fl oz (230 ml) Irish coffee
   glass

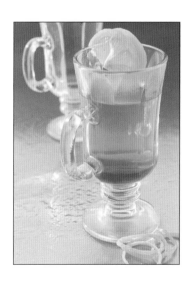

Pour the liquid ingredients and ¼ cup (50 ml) boiling water
into an Irish coffee glass and stir well. Garnish with the
lemon twist.

serves 1

Calypso Coffee

INGREDIENTS
slice of orange
sugar
1½ fl oz (45 ml) dark rum
hot coffee

whipped cream

GLASS
7½ fl oz (230 ml) Irish coffee
glass

Rub rim of glass with orange and frost with sugar. Pour rum into the glass and fill to within ½ in (15 mm) of the top with the hot coffee. Cover the surface with whipped cream.

serves 1

Chocolate Vice

INGREDIENTS
1½ fl oz (45 ml) dark rum
½ fl oz (15 ml) Bourbon
½ fl oz (15 ml) dark crème de cacao
4 fl oz (120 ml) hot chocolate

2 fl oz (60 ml) double (heavy) cream
chocolate flakes, to decorate

GLASS
7½ fl oz (230 ml) Irish coffee
glass

Pour first four ingredients into a mug, then carefully spoon cream on top. Sprinkle with chocolate flakes.

serves 1

Coffee Royal

INGREDIENTS
4 fl oz (120 ml) hot coffee
1 tsp (5 ml) granulated (white)
    sugar
2 fl oz (60 ml) brandy
2 fl oz (60 ml) double (heavy)
    cream

GLASS
7½ fl oz (230 ml) Irish coffee
    glass

Pour coffee into the glass, add sugar, stir to dissolve. Add the
brandy and stir well. Pour the cream carefully on top so that
it floats.

serves 1

Gin Toddy

INGREDIENTS
1 sugar cube
2 fl oz (60 ml) gin
slice of lemon, to garnish
ground (powdered) nutmeg,
    to garnish

GLASS
7½ fl oz (230 ml) hot wine mug

Place the sugar cube in the glass, pour over ½ cup (120 ml)
hot water and stir well, then add gin. Float the lemon slice on
top and sprinkle over nutmeg.

serves 1

Hot Brandy Alexander

INGREDIENTS

1 fl oz (30 ml) brandy
1 fl oz (30 ml) dark crème de
  cacao
4 fl oz (120 ml) hot (but not
  boiling) milk

whipped cream, to decorate
chocolate flakes, to decorate

GLASS
7½ fl oz (230 ml) Irish coffee
  glass

Pour all the ingredients except for the cream and chocolate
into a heated mug. Top with whipped cream and sprinkle with
chocolate flakes.

serves 1

Hot Buttered Rum

INGREDIENTS

1 tsp (5 ml) brown sugar
4 tsp (20 ml) butter
2 fl oz (55 ml) dark rum
ground (powdered) nutmeg

GLASS
7½ fl oz (230 ml) hot coffee
  mug

Place sugar in mug, pour over ½ cup (120 ml) hot water and
stir well, then add butter and rum. Sprinkle nutmeg on top.

serves 1

Hot Piper

INGREDIENTS
2 fl oz (60 ml) tequila
2 tsp (10 ml) lemon juice
½ fl oz (15 ml) dark crème
 de cacao
4 fl oz (120 ml) hot coffee

GLASS
7½ fl oz (230 ml) Irish coffee
 glass

Pour all ingredients into the Irish coffee glass and stir well.

serves 1

Hot Whisky Toddy

INGREDIENTS
1 sugar cube
2 fl oz (60 ml) Scotch whisky
slice of lemon, to decorate

GLASS
7½ fl oz (230 ml) hot whisky
 glass

Put sugar into glass, pour in ⅔ cup (150 ml) boiling water, then add whisky and stir. Decorate with a lemon slice.

serves 1

Indian Summer

INGREDIENTS
ground (powdered) cinnamon
2 fl oz (60 ml) Calvados
¾ cup (6 fl oz/175 ml) hot apple
    cider
1 cinnamon stick, to decorate

GLASS
7½ fl oz (230 ml) hot coffee
    mug

Dip rim of glass in ground cinnamon. Pour Calvados and cider
into mug, then add cinnamon stick.

serves 1

Irish Coffee

INGREDIENTS
slice of orange
sugar
1½ fl oz (45 ml) Irish whiskey
hot coffee
whipped cream

GLASS
7½ fl oz (230 ml) Irish coffee
    glass

Rub rim of glass with orange and frost with sugar. Pour Irish
whiskey into glass and fill to within ½ in (15 mm) of top with
the hot coffee. Cover surface to brim with whipped cream.

serves 1

Jamaican Coffee

INGREDIENTS
slice of orange
sugar
1½ fl oz (45 ml) Tia Maria
hot coffee
whipped cream

GLASS
7½ fl oz (230 ml) hot coffee
mug

Rub rim of glass with orange and frost with sugar. Pour Tia Maria into glass and fill to within ½ in (15 mm) of top with the hot coffee. Cover surface to brim with whipped cream.

serves 1

Mulled Claret

INGREDIENTS
1 sugar cube
5 fl oz (145 ml) claret
1½ tsp (7.5 ml) lemon juice
2 dashes of orange bitters
ground (powdered) cinnamon

GLASS
7½ fl oz (230 ml) hot coffee
mug

Stir the sugar into ¼ cup (50 ml) boiling water until dissolved. Stir in the remaining ingredients and mull with a red-hot spoon before serving.

serves 1

Long Drinks

The sophistication and drama of presenting long drinks at a cocktail party is both high in visual impact and practical, in that it can take the pressure off while getting the gathering into full swing. A tall drink will give your guests enough in their glass to hold on to and sip as they take the time to chat and unwind, leaving you time to prepare snacks, finger food or some smaller, more complicated cocktails as a follow up.

Astronaut

INGREDIENTS
2 fl oz (60 ml) dark rum
2 fl oz (60 ml) vodka
½ fl oz (15 ml) lemon juice
1 tsp (5 ml) passionfruit pulp

GLASS
9 fl oz (285 ml) hi-ball glass

Shake all the ingredients except passionfruit pulp with ice, and strain into glass. Drop passionfruit pulp into the glass.

serves 1

Bahama Mama

INGREDIENTS
½ fl oz (15 ml) light rum
½ fl oz (15 ml) Malibu
½ fl oz (15 ml) banana liqueur
½ fl oz (15 ml) grenadine
2 fl oz (60 ml) orange juice

2 fl oz (60 ml) pineapple juice
wedge of pineapple, to garnish

GLASS
9 fl oz (285 ml) hi-ball glass

Blend the liquid ingredients with ice and pour into the glass. Garnish with the pineapple wedge and serve with a straw.

serves 1

Blue Bayou

INGREDIENTS
1 fl oz (30 ml) gin
½ fl oz (15 ml) Galliano
½ fl oz (15 ml) dry vermouth
½ fl oz (15 ml) blue curaçao
lemonade

slice of lemon, to garnish
mint leaves, to garnish

GLASS
9 fl oz (285 ml) highball glass

Shake the first 4 ingredients over ice and pour into glass. Top up with lemonade. Garnish with the lemon slice and mint leaves. Serve with a straw.

serves 1

Blue French

INGREDIENTS
1 fl oz (30 ml) Pernod
½ fl oz (15 ml) blue curaçao
½ fl oz (15 ml) lemon juice
bitter lemon soda
slice of lemon, to garnish

GLASS
9 fl oz (285 ml) hi-ball glass

Build over ice in the glass. Top up with bitter lemon soda and stir well. Garnish with the lemon slice. Serve with a stirrer.

serves 1

Bombay Punch

INGREDIENTS
1 fl oz (30 ml) Cognac
½ fl oz (15 ml) dry sherry
½ fl oz (15 ml) Cointreau
½ fl oz (15 ml) maraschino
   liqueur
½ fl oz (15 ml) lemon juice
sparkling wine
1 red cherry, to garnish

GLASS
9 fl oz (285 ml) hi-ball glass

Blend the first 5 ingredients with ice and pour into the glass.
Top up with sparkling wine and garnish with the red cherry.
Serve with a straw.

serves 1

Brandy Ice

INGREDIENTS
1 fl oz (30 ml) brandy
½ fl oz (15 ml) vanilla extract
2 scoops vanilla ice cream
½ fl oz (15 ml) lemon juice
bitter lemon soda
slice of orange, to garnish
1 strawberry, to garnish

GLASS
9 fl oz (285 ml) hi-ball glass

Blend the first 4 ingredients with ice and pour into the glass.
Top up with bitter lemon soda and garnish with the orange
slice and strawberry. Serve with a straw and stirrer.

serves 1

Canadian Daisy

INGREDIENTS
1 fl oz (30 ml) Canadian Club
    whisky
½ fl oz (15 ml) brandy
½ fl oz (15 ml) lemon juice
1 tsp (5 ml) grenadine

soda water
1 cherry, to garnish

GLASS
9 fl oz (285 ml) hi-ball glass

Shake the first 4 ingredients with ice and pour into glass. Top
up with soda water and garnish with the cherry. Serve with a
straw and stirrer.

serves 1

Chi Chi

INGREDIENTS
1½ fl oz (45 ml) vodka
½ fl oz (15 ml) coconut cream
1 fl oz (30 ml) Malibu
½ fl oz (15 ml) lime syrup
½ fl oz (15 ml) lemon syrup

2 fl oz (60 ml) pineapple juice
whipped cream
pineapple wedge, to garnish

GLASS
9 fl oz (285 ml) hi-ball glass

Blend liquid ingredients with ice until smooth then pour into
glass. Garnish with the pineapple wedge. Serve with a straw
and stirrer.

serves 1

Chiquita

INGREDIENTS
1½ fl oz (45 ml) vodka
½ fl oz (15 ml) banana liqueur
½ fl oz (15 ml) lime juice
½ banana, sliced

pinch of sugar
bitter lemon soda

GLASS
9 fl oz (285 ml) hi-ball glass

Blend the first 5 ingredients with ice and pour into the glass.
Top up with bitter lemon soda. Serve with a straw.

serves 1

Dizzy Blonde

INGREDIENTS
2 fl oz (60 ml) advocaat
1 fl oz (30 ml) Pernod
lemonade
slice of orange, to garnish

GLASS
9 fl oz (285 ml) hi-ball glass

Shake the first 2 ingredients with ice and pour into the glass.
Top up with lemonade and garnish with the orange slice.
Serve with a straw and stirrer.

serves 1

Frangelico Luau

INGREDIENTS

1½ fl oz (45 ml) Frangelico
7 fl oz (200 ml) pineapple juice
dash of grenadine
slice of pineapple, to garnish

GLASS

9 fl oz (285 ml) hi-ball glass

Blend the first 3 ingredients with ice and pour into the glass.
Garnish with pineapple slice.

serves 1

Freddy Fud Pucker

INGREDIENTS

1 fl oz (30 ml) tequila
4 fl oz (120 ml) orange juice
½ fl oz (15 ml) Galliano
slice of orange, to garnish
1 cherry, to garnish

GLASS

9 fl oz (285 ml) hi-ball glass

Build over ice in the glass and float the Galliano on top.
Garnish with the orange slice and cherry.

serves 1

French 75

INGREDIENTS
1 fl oz (30 ml) gin
2 fl oz (60 ml) sweet-and-sour
    mix (see introduction)
Champagne

GLASS
9 fl oz (285 ml) hi-ball glass

Build over ice in the glass and stir lightly. Top up with
Champagne.

serves 1

Mai Tai

INGREDIENTS
1 fl oz (30 ml) white rum
½ fl oz (15 ml) amaretto
½ fl oz (15 ml) dark rum
1 fl oz (30 ml) orange curaçao
1 fl oz (30 ml) lemon juice
1 fl oz (30 ml) sugar syrup (see
    introduction)

½ fl oz (15 ml) lime juice
wedge of pineapple, to garnish
mint leaves, to garnish

GLASS
9 fl oz (285 ml) hurricane glass

Shake the liquid ingredients with ice and pour into the glass.
Garnish with the pineapple wedge and mint leaves. Serve with
a straw.

serves 1

Midori Matadors

INGREDIENTS
3 fl oz (90 ml) Midori
2 tsp (10 ml) caster (superfine)
    sugar
2 fl oz (60 ml) silver tequila
1 fl oz (30 ml) triple sec

2 lemon wedges, to garnish
3 fl oz (90 ml) lemon juice

GLASS
8 fl oz (250 ml) cocktail glass

Combine all ingredients, except the garnish, in a cocktail shaker and shake well. Fill the glasses with ice cubes. Strain the cocktail into the glasses evenly. Squeeze a lemon wedge into each glass and then drop the wedge into the glass to serve.

serves

Piña Colada

INGREDIENTS
1 fl oz (30 ml) light rum
1 fl oz (30 ml) coconut cream
2 fl oz (60 ml) pineapple syrup
1 pineapple spear, to garnish

GLASS
9 fl oz (285 ml) hi-ball glass

Blend the first 3 ingredients with ice until mixed, then pour into the glass. Garnish with a pineapple spear and serve with a straw.

serves 1

Planter's Punch

INGREDIENTS

1 fl oz (30 ml) dark rum
½ fl oz (15 ml) grenadine
dash of Angostura bitters
1½ fl oz (45 ml) sweet-and-sour
    mix (see introduction)
soda water
1 cherry, to garnish

GLASS

9 fl oz (285 ml) hi-ball glass

Shake the first 4 ingredients over ice and strain into the glass.
Top up with soda water and stir. Garnish with the cherry.
Serve with a straw and stirrer.

serves 1

Rocket Fuel

INGREDIENTS

ice
½ fl oz (15 ml) white rum
½ fl oz (15 ml) dry gin
½ fl oz (15 ml) vodka
½ fl oz (15 ml) tequila
1 fl oz (30 ml) lemonade

GLASS

8 fl oz (250 ml) cocktail glass

Fill the glass with ice and build the cocktail using the
ingredients in order. Serve with a straw and swizzle stick.

serves 1

Salty Dog

INGREDIENTS
lime wedge
salt
2 fl oz (60 ml) vodka
5 fl oz (145 ml) grapefruit juice

GLASS
9 fl oz (285 ml) hi-ball glass

Rub the lime wedge around the rim of the glass, then frost with salt. Almost fill the glass with ice cubes and pour the vodka and grapefruit juice into the glass. Stir well.

serves 1

Sex on the Beach

INGREDIENTS
1 fl oz (30 ml) vodka
2 fl oz (60 ml) cranberry juice
1 fl oz (30 ml) peach schnapps
2 fl oz (60 ml) orange juice

orange slice, to garnish

GLASS
9 fl oz (285 ml) hi-ball glass

Combine all the liquid ingredients in a glass filled with ice cubes and stir well. Garnish with the orange slice.

serves 1

Shady Lady

INGREDIENTS
ice cubes
1½ fl oz (45 ml) tequila
1½ fl oz (45 ml) melon liqueur
5 fl oz (145 ml) grapefruit juice,
    freshly squeezed

GLASS
9 fl oz (285 ml) hi-ball glass

Pour all of the ingredients into a hi-ball glass almost filled with ice cubes and stir well.

serves 1

Singapore Sling

INGREDIENTS
1 fl oz (30 ml) gin
2 fl oz (60 ml) sweet-and-sour
    mix (see introduction)
½ fl oz (15 ml) grenadine
½ fl oz (15 ml) cherry brandy
1 cherry, to decorate

GLASS
9 fl oz (285 ml) hi-ball glass

Build the first 3 ingredients over ice in glass and stir well. Top with cherry brandy and garnish with the cherry. Serve with a stirrer.

serves 1

Tom Collins

INGREDIENTS
2 fl oz (60 ml) lemon juice
1 tsp (5 ml) sugar
2 fl oz (60 ml) gin
soda water
slice of lemon, to garnish
1 cherry, to garnish

GLASS
9 fl oz (285 ml) hi-ball glass

Build the first 3 ingredients over ice in the glass and stir. Top up with soda water, garnish with the lemon slice and cherry. Serve with a straw and stirrer.

serves 1

Vodka Collins

INGREDIENTS
2 fl oz (60 ml) vodka
1 fl oz (30 ml) lemon juice
1 tsp (5 ml) caster (superfine)
    sugar
3 fl oz (90 ml) club soda

maraschino cherry, to garnish
orange slice, to garnish

GLASS
9 fl oz (285 ml) hi-ball glass

Combine first three ingredients in a cocktail shaker with cracked ice. Shake well and strain into a glass almost filled with clean ice cubes. Add the club soda and stir. Garnish with the cherry and orange slice.

serves 1

Wines &
Punches

Everyone loves a glass of dressed-up Champagne, a spiced wine or a cool summer spritzer. If you are planning for a larger gathering, it can also be a good strategy to provide some extra drinks where guests can help themselves from the pitcher or punch bowl at their leisure. Punches are another variety of drinks that are greatly enhanced by the use of fresh seasonal fruit – even though they are about to be soused, the better quality of fruit you add to a punch, the better the punch will taste.

Brazil Cocktail

INGREDIENTS
1½ fl oz (45 ml) dry sherry
1½ fl oz (45 ml) dry vermouth
dash of Angostura bitters
½ tsp (2.5 ml) ouzo

GLASS
5 fl oz (145 ml) tumbler

Place all the ingredients in the mixing glass with cracked ice, stir well and then strain into the cocktail glass.

serves 1

Buck's Fizz

INGREDIENTS
5 fl oz (145 ml) Champagne
½ fl oz (15 ml) Cointreau
1 fl oz (30 ml) orange juice
1½ tsp (7.5 ml grenadine
slice of orange, to garnish

GLASS
7 fl oz (200 ml) Champagne
  flute

Pour all ingredients except grenadine and orange slice into a chilled Champagne flute. Drop the grenadine into the centre of the drink and stir well. Garnish with the orange slice and serve with a straw.

serves 1

Claret Cobbler

INGREDIENTS
1 tsp (5 ml) caster (superfine) sugar
2 fl oz (60 ml) soda water
3 fl oz (90 ml) claret
1 red grape, to decorate

GLASS
7 fl oz (200 ml) red wine glass

Put the sugar in the glass and pour over the soda water. Stir until dissolved. Add the claret, then fill glass with cracked ice and stir well. Serve with the grape on the side of the glass.

serves 1

Easter Bonnet

INGREDIENTS
1½ fl oz (45 ml) apricot brandy
2 fl oz (60 ml) vodka
½ fl oz (15 ml fresh lime juice
Champagne
slice of lime, to decorate

1 pineapple spear, to decorate

GLASS
9 fl oz (230 ml) hurricane glass

Build over ice in hee glass, top up with Champagne and stir slowly. Garnish with lime and pineapple. Serve with a straw.

serves 1

Kir

INGREDIENTS
½ fl oz (15 ml) crème de cassis
dry white wine

GLASS
5 fl oz (145 ml) white wine glass

Pour crème de cassis into the glass, then top up with chilled dry white wine. Serve straight up.

serves 1

Kir Royal

INGREDIENTS
½ fl oz (15 ml) crème de cassis
Champagne

GLASS
5 fl oz (145 ml) Champagne
flute

Pour crème de cassis into glass, then top up with chilled Champagne. Serve straight up.

NOTE
Kir Imperial is made with grenadine and crème de cassis and Champagne.

serves 1

Port Cocktail

INGREDIENTS
2½ fl oz (75 ml) port
1½ tsp (7.5 ml) brandy

GLASS
5 fl oz (145 ml) cocktail glass

Place the ingredients in the mixing glass with cracked ice, stir well, then strain into cocktail glass.

serves 1

Spritzer

INGREDIENTS
3 fl oz (90 ml) dry white wine
soda water

GLASS
6 fl oz (180 ml) white wine glass

Pour chilled wine into the glass, then top up with chilled soda water, no ice.

serves 1

Twelfth Night Champagne

INGREDIENTS
slice of lime
caster (superfine) sugar
1 fl oz (30 ml) Grand Marnier
½ slice of lemon, to garnish
½ slice of orange, to garnish

dry Champagne

GLASS
5 fl oz (145 ml) Champagne
   flute

Rub lime slice around the rim of the Champagne flute, then frost the rim of the glass with sugar. Pour Grand Marnier into the glass, drop the slices of fruit in and top up with chilled Champagne.

serves 1

Apple Punch

INGREDIENTS
8 apples, cored and sliced
juice of 1 lemon
1¼ fl oz (40 ml) sugar
4 fl oz (120 ml) Calvados
2 bottles white wine

1 bottle soda water
1 bottle Champagne

SERVING BOWL
1 large punch bowl

Place apples in the punch bowl, drizzle lemon juice over and sprinkle with sugar. Refrigerate for 3–4 hours. Add the Calvados and white wine and stir well. Add the soda water, Champagne and 4 cups ice cubes. Serve in cocktail glasses or Champagne flutes.

serves 1

Cold Duck

INGREDIENTS

2 bottles white wine
1 bottle sparkling wine
2 lemon peel spirals, to garnish

SERVING BOWL

1 large punch bowl

Pour all ingredients into punch bowl with 2 cups ice cubes and stir well. Serve in Champagne flutes or white wine glasses.

serves 10

Gin Punch

INGREDIENTS

1 bottle gin
2 pints (1.2 litres) pineapple juice
2 pints (1.2 litres) lemonade
2 fl oz (60 ml) lemon juice
1¾ pints (1 litre) orange juice
selection of chopped fruit

SERVING BOWL

1 large punch bowl

Pour all ingredients into punch bowl with 4 cups ice cubes and stir well. Serve in punch cups.

serves 10

Kiwi Punch

INGREDIENTS
6 kiwi fruit, peeled and diced
2 nectarines, diced
1 fl oz (30 ml) dark rum
1 bottle dry white wine

1¾ pints (1 litre) lemonade

SERVING BOWL
1 large punch bowl

Place the fruit into the punch bowl, pour the rum over the fruit, then cover and refrigerate for about 1 hour. Add wine and stir well. Add 4 cups ice cubes, then top up with the lemonade. Serve in wine glasses or punch mugs.

serves 10

Melon Punch

INGREDIENTS
½ bottle melon liqueur
½ bottle vodka
1¾ pints (1 litre) lemonade
16 fl oz (475 ml) pineapple juice
selection of chopped fruit

SERVING BOWL
1 large punch bowl

Pour all ingredients into punch bowl with 2 cups ice cubes and stir well. Serve in white wine glasses.

serves 10

Old English Punch

INGREDIENTS
2 bunches mint leaves
8 fl oz (250 ml) whisky
2 bottles white wine
2 bottles Champagne

selection of chopped fruit

SERVING BOWL
1 large punch bowl

Crumble mint leaves and place them in the bowl with 4 cups ice cubes, pour the whisky over and let stand for about 15 minutes. Pour all other ingredients into the punch bowl and stir well. Serve in cocktail glasses.

serves 10

Pineapple Punch

INGREDIENTS
1 pineapple, peeled, cored
    and diced
1 lime, sliced
2 fl oz (60 ml) blue curaçao
2 fl oz (60 ml) dark rum

2 bottles dry white wine
1 bottle Champagne

SERVING BOWL
1 large punch bowl

Place the pineapple, lime, curaçao, rum and one bottle of white wine into the punch bowl, cover and refrigerate for about 3–4 hours. Add second bottle of wine and stir well. Add 4 cups ice cubes, then top up with the Champagne. Serve in cocktail glasses.

serves 10

Raspberry Lime Punch

INGREDIENTS

1 lb (450 g) raspberries
1 lime, sliced
40 g (1¾ oz) caster (superfine)
   sugar

2 bottles rosé wine
3 bottles Champagne

SERVING BOWL

1 large punch bowl

Place raspberries and lime slices into punch bowl. Sprinkle sugar over the fruit, cover and refrigerate for about half an hour. Add rosé and stir well. Add 4 cups ice cubes, then top up with the Champagne. Serve in cocktail glasses.

serves 10

Sangria

INGREDIENTS

1 bottle claret
2 fl oz (60 ml) brandy
2 fl oz (60 ml) white rum
2 fl oz (60 ml) Cointreau
1¾ pints (1 litre) orange juice

2 tsp (10 ml) sugar
selection of chopped fruit

SERVING BOWL

1 large punch bowl

Pour all ingredients into punch bowl with 4 cups ice cubes and stir well. Serve in cocktail glasses.

serves 10

Non-Alcoholic

For the health conscious or for children – or just for some delicious alternatives to all that booze – here we provide you with a range of non-alcoholic drinks worthy for inclusion at a cocktail party. It is always good to provide refreshments that are as sophisticated as cocktails but will leave your guests clear-headed as they leave to make their way home. Also, if you are planning a lunch or early afternoon party, it is good to have quenching refreshments around so that the entire day remains an elegant affair.

Alice in Wonderland

INGREDIENTS
3½ fl oz (100 ml) grapefruit
  juice
1 fl oz (30 ml) green tea
4 tsp (20 ml) lemon juice
½ fl oz (15 ml) sugar syrup (see
  introduction)

soda water
1 grape

GLASS
6 fl oz (180 ml) tulip cocktail
  glass

Build over ice and top up with soda water. Garnish with a
grape.

serves 1

Banapple Smoothie

INGREDIENTS
4 fl oz (120 ml) milk
½ banana, sliced
½ apple, peeled
½ cup natural (plain) yogurt
1 tsp (5 ml) honey

2–3 drops vanilla extract
sprinkles

GLASS
¾ pint (460 ml) fancy hi-ball
  glass

Place all ingredients, except sprinkles and 1–2 slices of banana,
in blender with 3 ice cubes and blend until smooth. Pour
into chilled glass, garnish with sprinkles and reserved banana
and serve.

serves 1

Banana Zing Smoothie

INGREDIENTS
4 fl oz (120 ml) milk
½ banana
juice of 1 orange
3–4 drops lemon juice
4 fl oz (120 ml) natural (plain)
    yogurt
2 tsp (10 ml) apple juice
    concentrate
slice of orange, to garnish

GLASS
¾ pint (460 ml) hurricane glass

Place all ingredients except orange slice in blender with four ice cubes and blend until smooth. Pour into chilled glass and serve topped with a slice of orange and a straw.

serves 1

Banberry Smoothie

INGREDIENTS
4 fl oz (120 ml) milk
½ banana
2 strawberries
½ apple, peeled
5–6 blueberries
4 fl oz (120 ml) natural (plain)
    yogurt
1 tsp (5 ml) honey
orange slice, to decorate

GLASS
9 fl oz (285 ml) old-fashioned
    glass

Place all ingredients except orange slice in blender with four ice cubes and blend until smooth. Pour into chilled glass and serve topped with a slice of orange and a straw.

serves 1

Berry Banana Smoothie

INGREDIENTS
6 frozen strawberries
10–12 blueberries
4 fl oz (120 ml) milk
1 banana
1 tsp (5 ml) honey

2 drops vanilla extract
vanilla sugar

GLASS
¾ pint (460 ml) hi-ball glass

Reserve one strawberry and a few blueberries. Place all remaining ingredients except sugar in blender with four ice cubes and blend until smooth. Pour into chilled glass and serve topped with reserved strawberry and blueberries, and a sprinkle of vanilla sugar.

serves 1

Blunt Screwdriver

INGREDIENTS
4 fl oz (120 ml) ginger ale
4 fl oz (120 ml) orange juice
slice of orange

1 red cherry

GLASS
9 fl oz (285 ml) hi-ball glass

Build over ice. Garnish with the orange slice and red cherry.

NOTE
This cousin of the well-known alcoholic screwdriver substitutes the ginger ale for vodka. Add ½ fl oz (15 ml) grenadine for a Roy Rogers.

serves 1

Calypso Smoothie

INGREDIENTS
pulp of 3 passionfruit
4 fl oz (120 ml) milk
2½ fl oz (75 ml) pineapple juice
½ banana
½ cup natural (plain) yogurt

1 tsp (5 ml) honey

GLASS
¾ pint (460 ml) hurricane glass

Reserve the pulp of 1 passionfruit. Place all remaining ingredients in a blender with 4 ice cubes and blend until smooth. Pour into a chilled glass and serve with a swirl of passionfruit pulp to garnish.

serves 1

Cranberry Zinger

INGREDIENTS
4 fl oz (120 ml) cranberry juice
2 tsp (10 ml) brown sugar
1 tsp (5 ml) lemon extract
1 cup pineapple pieces
8 fl oz (250 ml) ginger ale

GLASS
9 fl oz (285 ml) hi-ball glass

Combine all the ingredients except the ginger ale. Add the ginger ale and ice before serving.

serves 2

Ginger Mick

INGREDIENTS
4 fl oz (120 ml) dry ginger ale
½ fl oz (15 ml) lime juice
1 fl oz (30 ml) Claytons tonic
1 fl oz (30 ml) lemon juice

60 ml apple juice
slice of banana

GLASS
9 fl oz (285 ml) hi-ball glass

Blend the liquid ingredients with ice and pour into the glass.
Garnish with banana slices wedged on the rim of the glass.

serves 1

Mockatin

INGREDIENTS
½ fl oz (15 ml) lime juice
dash of lemon juice
2 fl oz (60 ml) tonic water

1 green olive

GLASS
3 fl oz (90 ml) cocktail glass

Stir liquid ingredients with ice and strain. Garnish with a green
olive on a toothpick or a lemon twist.

serves 1

Shirley Temple

INGREDIENTS
½ fl oz (15 ml) grenadine
8 ½ fl oz (270 ml) ginger ale or
   lemonade
slice of orange

GLASS
9 fl oz (285 ml) hi-ball glass

Build over ice. Garnish with the slice of orange.

NOTE: For a tangy variation to this drink, try a Shirley Temple No.2. Use 2 fl oz (60 ml) pineapple juice to a glass half-full of ice. Top with lemonade, float ½ fl oz (15 ml) passionfruit pulp on top and garnish with a pineapple wedge and cherry.

serves 1

Strawberry Swirl

INGREDIENTS
4 frozen strawberries
ground (powdered) cinnamon
4 tablespoons strawberry
   topping

8 fl oz (250 ml) milk

GLASS
9 fl oz (285 ml) hi-ball glass

Place strawberries, cinnamon, 1 ice cube and half the strawberry topping into a blender and blend until puréed. Put in the freezer in a small bowl while you make the rest of the drink. Without rinsing the blender, add the milk and remaining strawberry topping and blend until frothy. Spoon the frozen pulp into the bottom of the glass and drizzle a little extra syrup around the sides. Pour over the strawberry milkshake and serve.

serves 1

INDEX

First published in 2013 by
New Holland Publishers
London • Sydney • Cape Town • Auckland
www.newhollandpublishers.com

The Chandlery Unit 114 50 Westminster Bridge Road London SE1 7QY
1/66 Gibbes Street Chatswood NSW 2067 Australia
Wembley Square First Floor Solan Road Gardens Cape Town 8001 South Africa
218 Lake Road Northcote Auckland New Zealand

A catalogue record of this book is available at the British Library and at the National Library of Australia

ISBN: 9781742574806

10 9 8 7 6 5 4 3 2 1

Texture: Shutterstock photo

Publisher: Fiona Schultz
Designer: Lorena Susak
Photographer: Brent Parker Jones
Production director: Olga Dementiev
Printer: Toppan Leefung Printing Limited

Follow New Holland Publishers on
Facebook: www.facebook.com/NewHollandPublishers